WAi
CAUCASUS

GEORGIA

by
Peter Nasmyth

LONDON 2006

To,
David,

with best wishes

MTA Publications

Published by Mta Publications
Email: mtapublications@yahoo.co.uk

Distributed by I.B.Tauris & Co.Ltd
6 Salem Road, London W2 4BU
175 Fifth Avenue, New York NY 10010
Email: mail@ibtauris.com
www.ibtauris.com

ISBN 1-84511-206-7

Every attempt has been made to make the information in this book reliable and accurate. The publishers would be happy to receive any comments and suggestions toward improvement.

Design by Kakha Bakhtadze   Email: kakha@gccw.org

All photographs © Peter Nasmyth, unless otherwise stated.
Cover Photograph Mt Ushba, Svaneti.

ACKNOWLEDGEMENTS

This book would not have happened without the help of many good friends, old and new – all with similar commitments to Georgia's fine landscape. Every name carries either a long association or recent dedication, meriting a paragraph apiece. It feels wrong to merely list them, but still…. The two Kakha Bakhtadzes, Nino Chanturia, Marika Didebulidze, Rupert Earle, Nick Erkomaishvili, Ramas Gokhelashvili, Tony Harner, Mamuka Japaridze, George Kalandadze, Saba Kiknadze, Iain Lunt, Tako Megrelishvili, Nutsa Megvinetukhutsesi, Giorgi Mikeladze, Natia Mouladze, Bakur Salukauri, Amy Spurling, Karin Steinmetzer, Servane Laine, Iya Tabaguri, Darren Woodcock, John Wright. This is an incomplete list and omits many long suffering guides, and fellow walkers who accompanied me through these mini-adventures.

The book is dedicated to Zaliko Kikodze

CONTENTS

.A Svanetian host

INTRODUCTION

It has always surprised me how so many people come to Georgia, admire the churches, caves towns, song, dance and cuisine – yet never visit the mountains. This is rather like touring Switzerland without visiting the Alps. But with some encouragement, this hopefully may soon change. For the Greater Caucasus are not only the centre-piece of this small but very beautiful, country, their physical presence is arguably grander than the Alps, especially for those attracted to landscape and wildlife. Certainly the peaks are higher – six exceed 5000 metres - and the chain is longer, extending 1200kms between the Black and Caspian Seas. But more significantly, the high valleys are spotted with antique stone towers, hill-top churches and numerous long-inhabited villages. Those who live in these fabulously remote places are the progeny of two thousand years of conquest and survival – and famed for their hospitality. With such a landscape, history and people it would be strange indeed if the Caucasus were *not* a superb walker's destination.

They are, of course. Furthermore Georgia, the country set in their geographical heart, contains more native flora and fauna, plus endemic birds than any in Europe (if Russia, the biggest country in the world is excluded). This is explained by Georgia's extraordinary landscape diversity, which ranks in the world's top twelve. A remarkable fact considering its size - a mere 67,900 square km, an area the size of Ireland. But Georgia can boast a Black Sea coast, subtropical wetlands, semi-desert, volcanic plateaus (dormant), large areas of virgin forest, sub alpine and high alpine zones, topped by three 5000 metre peaks.

But these qualities of landscape are well matched by the culture that developed among them. The Caucasus mountains have seen consistent habitation and culturalisation from pre-historic periods. Set on the crucial land isthmus between what is now called Europe and Asia, this giant row of mountains forms not only a natural barrier but also a protective cloak for its local communities. Georgia has been invaded so many times, hosted armies of Greeks, Romans, Vikings, Mongols, Persians, Ottoman Turks, Russians, Armenians and even the British (who deposited 20,000 troops in Batumi in 1919). This constant external bombardment has forced whole communities up into the safety of high valleys so often – they developed a unique culture of preservation. Customs maintained themselves up in the highlands until the invading armies retreated down below - then they returned back down. Before the arrival of the Bolsheviks in 1921, over 50% of Georgia's population still lived within mountain areas. Since the Soviet relocations the figure today stands at less that 15%, but each region still maintains a distinctive character and life-style. As a result walkers will encounter extraordinary stone villages, towers, burial sites, some of great antiquity – in the remotest places.

To walk in Georgia is to have all this at one's fingertips - literally. Many of the finest walks in this book are just one and a half hour's drive from the capital, Tbilisi. All are set in a landscape largely unmolested by the leisure industry. Whether along the flanks of lower valleys or puffing up toward the eternal snows, the walker for the most part strides away into a landscape free of sign-posts and markers; warnings and wagging fingers. A place more attuned to natural law than human.

As for the **paths** – plentiful, well trodden, but mostly unmarked as walks per se – used by shepherds, cattle and sheep. Animals are herded up to pasture in the summer, then escorted down in the autumn. The question is rarely whether there is a path – but which one – hence this guide. Walking is still a novel occupation for many Georgians – 'why walk if you can take a jeep?' I'm often asked. The highest walk in this book touches 3200 metres (most vary between 1000 and 2500 metres), but unlike other walking environments, a good many can be extended upward at the walker's choice, to even more stupendous views.

Empty Hills

One factor in Georgia's relative freedom from tourism is a change in reputation thirteen years ago - from earthly Soviet paradise to 'dangerous' - an unfortunate, if effective tactic in landscape preservation. It comes thanks to a civil war in the early 1990s, after the collapse of the Soviet Union, then ongoing unresolved conflicts in Abkhazia, South Ossetia and neighbouring Chechnya. As a result its public image made a 180 degree turn and this walker's paradise is only just arriving back on the international hiker's map.

This book is for those able to see beyond the poorly researched news headlines ('Georgia, on the Brink of Civil War,' was a favourite during the bloodless Rose Revolution of 2003). Those who come are rewarded by some of the most stunning landscapes in Europe - with which these pages do little more than scratch the surface. For every walk noted here a dozen of equal quality remain un-charted around it.

Geology

To walk in the Caucasus is to place your feet onto a young, energetic geology. Below the ground the enormous forces of the Arabian tectonic plate continues to push the mountains upward while, one could say, on the surface human cultures generates a string of comparable dramas, wars, celebrations. Formed a mere 25 million years ago, the area of the Greater Caucasus mountains was once a sub-tropical island which, as the plates shifted, joined with land above and below, then compressed upward. The higher mountains (like Mts Ushba, Tetnuldi, Shkhara) have been dug and shaped by erosion - glacier, snow, wind and rivers. But the highest peak (Mt Elbruz at 5642 metres, just north of the Georgian border in Russia) is older and an ancient volcano (along with Mt Kazbek, 5033 metres). These two giants also stand as marker posts between its three geological areas - the Western, Central and Eastern Caucasus. The last two contain many of these walks and the Central most of the Caucasus's 2000 glaciers. The western half of the Central Caucasus is mostly granite and shale. It contains the highest peaks including Shkhara – Georgia's own highest at 5068 metres. The eastern section is generally andesite and diabase, with some granite outcrops. The Eastern Caucasus are slightly lower and drier, composed of argillaceous slate, sandstone, diabase, porphyrite. Below lies Georgia's fertile valleys, ranging from the sub-tropical Colchian lowlands in the west to the slightly higher, wine-producing Kakhetian valley of east Georgia. The country is divided in two by the ridge of Suram mountains roughly half way across Georgia's 800km-long landmass. Below these the Lesser Caucasus rise up (rarely exceeding 3000 metres) then descend down to the high plateau of Samtskhe-Javakheti of around 2000 metres along the southern border with Armenia and Turkey.

Mt Kazbek, at 5033 metres, is the most popular with mountaineers and rated as an easy 2B climb (Russian system – 6 is highest). First climbed in 1868 by Douglas Freshfield of the London Alpine Club, locals claimed a sacred tree adorned its summit with treasure spread around its base. However only the pure could see it. Needless to say the Alpine Club returned empty handed. Climbing to the summit takes four days, requires acclimatisation, a mountain guide, crampons, ice-walking and real fitness.

Personal note

W hy, I'm often asked, have I now written a walking guide, rather than a more in-depth cultural investigation? The answer is, not only because walking itself is a serious cultural investigation, but also, the longer I stay in Georgia, the more it seems that everything flows down from its mountains, culture included, With 40% of its landmass at over 900 metres, Georgia's heritage has retreated up into, then down from the high valleys too many times. To understand Georgia it's not enough simply to walk around the main cities and churches, one must enter those other great cathedrals – the canyons and peaks of the Greater Caucasus, meet their animals, birds and geology; sense the colours of flowers, the rushing rivers, drastic peaks, feel the atmosphere of urgency, sudden bursts of beauty and calamity – from which all the lowland culture emerges. People are often surprised by the number of 11th-12th century towers still standing in incredibly remote valleys. But to my mind, these are the essential stays of a modern Georgian culture. Attacked and defended; resisting snow, sun, sudden torrents, vendettas, their well-knitted stones survive on as a message from what lies behind their now crumbling facades. For instance the engaging and instant 'Georgian hospitality' we all enjoy, develops from this long history of conquest, attack and defence. Georgians learnt centuries ago that the best method of defence is making your enemies your friend. This remains as fundamental to the Georgian character as towers are to Svaneti and Tusheti. And, one hopes, long may it last.

WALKING NOTES
for the CAUCASUS

Walking Times

Walking-guide readers sometimes complain that quoted times don't fit their own speeds. However duration spent on the trail is still a useful indicator in mountainous areas where kilometres don't work – if explained. So, to be clear – these times are _mine_. I would describe myself as an average walker with early training in the fogs and bogs of Dartmoor. When fit I can sustain a couple of hours 'up' before taking a proper rest – except at altitudes over 2500 metres. However I take surreptitious rests via photo stops – so these walk-times are slightly on the slow side for the keen hiker. But they try to be realistic Caucasian times, not hurrying, competitive speeds. They include gaps for snacks, plenty of photo stops and greet-ings with the guide's friends/relatives along the way. If you're a fast-walker you can probably lop an hour off times over 4 hours – as I can never resist a good view.

Taking a guide

Taking guides is as good for conversation as for direction. On bigger walks you'd be advised to take one as well as this book. There are often several routes up the same pass (like the Guli pass in Svaneti). Some paths are wiped out by landslides in the spring but cattle quickly find new ways, so trails – of a sort – re-appear. By using common sense, the occasional question, the maps and landmarks in this guide, a way through will be found. In Svaneti be advised to take a local (Svan speaking) guide at all times – as a security bridge between yourselves and the people of this remote, poor and proudly independent culture.

9

Finding guides/hotels/general information

Websites now supply more up to date travel information than books. Below are some of the best - mostly from Tbilisi's local tourist companies. These are still small and friendly and try to continue a tradition that hails the guest as 'a gift from God.' Well experienced in organising guides/transport/accommodation (homestays and hotels), they're not a bad port of call at the start. I often employ them. Use guides well, ask plenty of questions, get to know them and Georgia's ancient culture, its habits, traditions, expectations.

'Caucasus Travel' **www.caucasustravel.com**

Email - georgia@caucasustravel.com
[The first western-style company to emerge after independence. Now the largest - which isn't big in Georgia. Still feels family-like and competent. I've used them many times.]

'Explore Georgia' **www.exploregeorgia.com**

Email - info@exploregeorgia.com
[Nick Erkomaishvili, most people's favourite mountain guide, now has his own company. Fortunately he's not chained himself to a desk.]

'Georgica Travel' **www.georgicatravel.ge**

Email - georgica@caucasus.net
[A Danish/Georgian joint venture, going strong. Good people, and I enjoy their company and loosing bets with Nino on Georgian history. Plenty of experience]

'Visit Georgia' **www.visitgeorgia.com**

Email - visitgeorgia@geo.net.ge
[A company with good connections to western European travel companies. I keep bumping into their tours in distant corners of Georgia]

'Wild Georgia' **www.wildgeorgia.ge**

Email – eka@wildgeorgia.ge
[Brand new company specialising in Tusheti - where it's 22 year old director, Eka, was its first ever woman riding champion and still 'dances on a horse.'

The Tourism Department has an excellent website including maps, history and accommodation right across Georgia;
www.tourism.gov.ge

Internet access, books, coffee, fellow walkers are found at **Prospero's Bookshop,** 34 Rustaveli. Tbilisi.

Maps

The excellent maps here are provided by Kakha Bakhtadze, a GIS specialist at the Caucasus Environmental NGO Network. He can be contacted at *kakha.bakhtadze@cenn.org*
Note: Some walker's routes - marked in green - may vary very slightly from those delineated, as they were plotted from memory. But Georgia will soon have its own GPS maps.

Directions and hospitality

In the Caucasus the walker's clock is turned back several decades. You're not bombarded by signs, safety symbols, park rangers and groups of other trekkers. Bar on a few well-marked, internationally funded walks (as in Borjomi), your wits are your best guide and often encounter the unexpected (see the 'Stories' below).
When asking for directions in the Caucasus you must be aware people rarely like to say they don't know. Nearly always they'll point somewhere, give some indication, even if they're not sure they understood you. They want to be helpful to guests – this is still a strong tradition, especially in the mountains. So watch their eyes carefully. If hesitant, be careful. In remoter places there is a chance you will be invited into houses for 'just a quick glass' that mysteriously blossoms into a full-blown toasting session (and sometimes meal) and lasts for over an hour. This has happened to me many times. It can be a pleasure, adding a bonus to a walk (if not in a hurry), but can also be a hazard – especially at the start of walks when you're not sure how much time is needed. On these occasions best to be friendly but firm. Smile graciously,

*ıinkali (meat or cheese
ımpling) waiting to be cooked
Shenakho, Tusheti*

apologise many times, say just about anything to show your potential host that only tiresome circumstance prevents you from taking up a fabulous invitation. This is important in the Caucasus due to the cult of hospitality. On several occasions I've come across locals standing around drinking and literally been unable to receive directions without first drinking a toast. If you're in this situation drink just one cup, ask for wine not spirits (there's usually both), hold up a glass, say a quick, bold toast about how beautiful ('lamazi') their village ('sopeli') and Georgia ('Sakartbelo') is, how they are good friends ('kargi megobari') and thank them sincerely ('didi maadloba') for their directions (which they have yet to give), then drain the glass in one. When they then re-fill it and hand it back – smile and politely refuse. Point at your watch, place your hand on your heart and ask again for directions. This invariably works. [See Walker's Words at end for key Georgian words in such an event]

Altitude and sickness

Altitude sickness is extremely rare at the heights attained in these walks. Officially the effects of altitude only kick in at 2500 metres – the top of most routes here. However altitude is definitely a factor when calculating times, especially on first arrival. If planning high walks, say around Kazbegi or in Svaneti, the less fit should do the lower walks first or be prepared to slow right down as the metres mount. I need about three days to acclimatise. First signs of acute mountain sickness (AMS) are 'breathlessness, headaches, nausea,' (often experienced anyway!). If when you stop and rest they don't disappear within 10 minutes, you may be effected and should descend , which invariably effects a cure. Be aware that everyone acclimatises at different speeds and heights; that fitness is a factor in susceptibility. If concerned there is a drug – Acetazolamide (Diamox), which can be carried.

Fitness

 Some walkers stepping straight out of offices have poor ideas about their fitness, until finding themselves struggling to keep up. They think because they go to the gym twice a week they're fit. Many walk simply to become fit. If so - go at it *sensibly*. Don't try to break records on the first day. Your body must acclimatise, muscles strengthen at their own speed. Furthermore, over-exertion can be dangerous – for the knees, ankles or heart.

Security

Unfortunately for the walking world, Georgia periodically acquires an exaggerated reputation as 'dangerous' because only bad news from small nations tends to make it into the international press. The entire Caucasus as 'war zone' is an image hard to shift, especially with the Chechen problem, Nagorno Karabakh, Abkhazia and Ossetia. The effect is to tar all of Georgia with the same brush and create a vague and grotesque phantom hanging over the country. Once visited the image evaporates, to be replaced by one of the most engaging walking environments in the world. However some areas are definitely safer than others. At one point robberies in the Svaneti region stopped all group-tourism. But some dramatic, surgical action by the new Georgian government improved matters enough for groups to return (individuals always went).

Fear however can ruin the enjoyment of any landscape – so be mentally prepared. Below are some points that help stay fear-free in Georgia.

- The sight of people carrying guns isn't uncommon; usually hunters or shepherds needing to protect their sheep.
- In Svaneti accompaniment by a local is advised – locals need to identify you with a local host family (your main protection). Strangers are mistrusted.
- In unexpected meetings that you feel could go either way – one policy is to offer whole hearted friendship. I often present a bold outstretched hand to the suspi-
- cious or unfriendly. This has worked on several occasions (see my book, 'Georgia, in the Mountains of Poetry' for examples).

Water

Remember that energetic walkers require up to three litres of water a day in cool conditions, six litres in hot or at high altitude. Springs are encountered on most of the mountain walks here. They save carrying heavy water bottles – but are easy to miss. Always check a spring isn't a stream – to be avoided below about 3100 metres as animals pasture very high in the Caucasus. Water straight from the glacier is usually OK.

Equipment

None of the walks in this book require transportation of tents/camping gear. They come with accommodation built in – mostly back at the point of origin. Heavy packs hinder progress and bring on a different attitude to walking. However indications for longer treks are given and a few of these routes are quite demanding, so proper hiking gear/shoes are essential. Remember once up in the Caucasus, little is available back at base. No convenient walkers' shops with maps, new shoes, GPS, rain/snow gear. Nature is more pristine so less protected from the dangers associated with a major mountain-range. Don't expect a helicopter to come chopping over the ridge after one mobile phone call. Although one risks listing the obvious – below are a few personal tips.

Rain Gear
Weather changes rapidly in any mountain environment. Even if the sky is totally blue when setting out, bring light, portable rain gear, including leggings.

Gaiters
If planning to go high, be prepared for patches of fresh snow - at any time of year. Locals often wear gumboots, which seems crazy at the start of the walk, but not when over 3000 metres plodding through snow fields, Gaiters are light and also useful waterproof seats.

Sun-cream/block/hat/glasses
The higher you go, the stronger the sun. Very important for the fair skinned. Sun burn is possible in the mountains at all times of year. Remember sun reflects UP from snow, so dose lower chin, nose, ear lobes. Sunglasses help against the glare.

Mobile phone (and Mobile signal)
Not essential – but comforting. Coverage is surprisingly good in Georgia's mountains even in remote areas (land lines are unreliable). Most mountain guides carry them. **Mobile signal** *here is the Magti system.*

Water-bottle
A small, light, re-fillable water bottle is useful – for the many springs in the Caucasus.

Mini Binoculars
Excellent not only for bird and animal spotting – but also for plotting the way forward; checking that one's current path doesn't abruptly terminate in a new landslide.

Hazardous animals/plants

The Caucasus are pretty safe. A few bears still survive in some of the large forested areas but due to extensive hunting are shy of humans (unlike the tourist-savvy American bears). Georgia has poisonous snakes [see **Animals** section] and scorpions like other hot countries – but they are rare. One exception is the sandy high-desert in Spring. However I've visited David Gareji many May/Junes and only seen one (non-poisonous) snake. Poison Ivy and Oak (plants with irritant leaves) don't exist in the Caucasus.

Dogs

The greatest annoyance to walkers in the Caucasus. Out of cities the large, clipped-eared, Caucasian dog is trained to defend flocks and homesteads. Anything approaching is barked-at determinedly. Not pleasant – although bites are extremely rare (rabies exists in Georgia but I've never seen it). The best way to deal with these large animals is to avoid them. When you see flocks of sheep or shepherd's homesteads, steer well away or attract the shepherd's attention, who will call them off. But even then be cautious, they don't like being nice. When confronted with aggressive, following dogs I walk on steadily, never meeting their eyes but holding a stick. Some people throw stones away from dogs – which they chase, but usually return; others carry pepper-spray. However don't panic and don't run. If they start snapping turn and confront them firmly. Shout, raise the stick while slowly making your retreat. Dogs have an invisible sense of territory. Once you're outside they let you go and return, happy for the sport, back to their sheep.

Avalanches, glaciers, bridges, river crossings

It is not uncommon when walking high, to come across avalanches (as in the Devdoraki valley). Better to cross these one by one – in the unlikely event of a collapse others can help you. Glaciers are more dangerous; they are alive, unpredictable and most require ropes. NEVER stand admiringly directly below the glacier tongue – rocks periodically hurtle down and can decapitate. Many of the home-made bridges across rivers are washed away in the spring. If there one year, they may not be the next (or re-appear further up or down). When wading rivers remember, if swift flowing, it's virtually impossible to cross beyond knee depth. The inexperienced can and do drown, often dragged under by their backpacks. I use a stick for stability – also on avalanches.

COUNTRY CODE

Forest fires are rare in the Caucasus – which could be due to the relatively low number of tourists. In the unlikely event you build a fire (not advised) be sure all embers are totally extinguished on departure – sudden winds can pick them up and start forest fires. Remember your walking paradise is many people's back yard, so take away your rubbish, close the gates and don't pick flowers/orchids (even though locals do).

Autumn in Bakuriani

adult male 'Jikhvi' - Western Caucasian

FLORA AND FAUNA

ANIMALS
with Insects and Reptiles

Georgia has more indigenous animals than any country in Europe – excluding Russia (the largest country in the world). A remarkable fact for such a small nation and explained by its wide landscape diversity and large areas of genuinely virgin forest. Today over 90% of Georgia's forest is still naturally planted. Wolves, brown bears, jackals, lynx and other predators are all found – not the case in most other European countries. The mountains are also home to many hoofed animals; roe deer, red deer, chamois, wild boar, wild or bezoar goat – but the real find is the endemic **Caucasian tur** or 'jikhvi' (related to the European Ibex), its two species still living in herds high in the Greater Caucasus. There are rumours that the **Anatolian Leopard** may be trying to return - an adult male was caught by remote cameras in the Vashlovani National Park in 2003. This beautiful but critically endangered animal - once found across the whole Caucasus and featuring in numerous legends and poems - was long thought-of as extinct in Georgia.

Wild Cat ('tkis kata'). Looks like a domestic cat, but larger and stronger (5-8 kilos). Grey/brown with spotted fur and ringed tail. Prefers lowland forests. Very hard to see, but footprints are common and sometimes you hear its 'meow.'

Red Deer ('ketilshobili iremi'). Magnificent animal, males with large 5 branched antlers (doe has none) – weighs up to 400kilos, found up to 3100 metres. Now very rare in Georgia, due to excessive hunting – only about 200 left. Protected.

Roe Deer ('shveli'). Half the size of the Red Deer. Fairly common in forests. Hunting permitted in Game Farms (Georgia has 20).

Lynx ('potskhveri'). A rare but splendid large cat (up to 24 kilos), found across the Caucasus up to about 2500 metres. To see one, even at a distance, is a real treat and extremely difficult. Georgian population declining; now about 150. Most frequent in forest and semiarid andscape. Protected.

Chamois ('archvi'). Now very rare due to poaching. Population down 75% in the last 20 years. Easily distinguished by its short black antlers, hooked at the tips. Graceful animal, can be found very high, at up to 4000 metres, adults weigh between 25 and 50 kilos. Protected.

Wolf ('mgeli'). Still widespread, up to 3500 metres, but eradicated from many low-land areas. They take sheep, hence employment of the Caucasian dog (larger and stronger) for protection. They are shy of humans and extremely unlikely to attack.

Caucasian Wild Goat ('niamori'). Similar to the Bezour Goat. Now only a few left of this handsome, bearded goat, mostly in Tusheti, up to 3500 metres. 50 to 80 kilos. Protected but in danger of extinction in Georgia due to poaching.

Jackal ('tura'). Occurs everywhere, including the edges of cities. The size of a medium-sized dog (up to 12 kilos), it moves at a trot. Common across Georgia but rarely seen above 1000 metres. Doesn't bark – whines.

Caucasian Tur ('jikhvi'). This fine high-altitude animal (recorded up to 4000 metres) comes in two species – West and East Caucasus. Georgia has both. Up to 80 kilos. Capra Caucasica (western) has longer, dramatically curled horns (much longer and more deeply curved than the European Ibex). Capra Cylindricornis (eastern) has shorter, more vertical horns. They are found nowhere else in the world. Endangered due to excessive hunting. Population halved since the 1980s to about 2500. On the IUCN Red List. Protected.

Wild Boar ('greuli khori'). Found in forests and semi-arid areas up to 1500 metres. Relatively common. Large; up to 150 kilos. Solo males can be aggressive, but rarely dangerous,

Brown Bear ('dartvi'). Much persecuted but still a few left – found in forested areas up to about 3500 metres. Very shy of humans but large (up to 300 kilos). Walks most of the time but can run fast and climb trees. If encountered walk away slowly (don't run). But in nearly every case it will see you first and make its own departure. If with cubs, never move between them and the mother. Protected.

REPTILES/AMPHIBIANS

Photo: David Tarkhnishvili

Lebetina Viper ('giusa'). Most common poisonous snake. Found only in eastern Georgia and mostly in sandy, rocky semi-desert (like David Gareji).

Caucasian Viper ('kavkasiuri gvelgesla'). Poisonous, endemic to the Caucasus and very rare. Up to 75 cm long. Found in high alpine forest. If you see one feel privileged!

Ring Snake ('chveulebrivi ankara') Georgia's most common snake. Easily identified by bright white or yellow strips on either side of its head. Non-poisonous.

Caucasian Salamander ('kavkasiuri salamandra'). A handsome black and yellow spotted small water-lizard, unique to the south  west Caucasus. Total length up to 17 cm. Prefers cool, humid gorges – like those in the Borjomi National Park.

Caucasian Agama ('jojo'). Medium-sized Caucasian lizard – up to 25cm head to tail. Quite common in stony areas of South East Georgia.

Mediterranean Turtle ('testudo greaca'). Claimed as endemic to Georgia. Common across Georgia, can grow up to a length of 40cms. Hibernates in winter, seen April to November, most frequently in the dry, sandy land-scapes of south Georgia.

INSECTS

Butterflies

Old World Swallowtail (Papilio Machaon). Found April/May and then July/September. Generally rare, but locally common. I've seen swarms in the Tbilisi Botanical Gardens, early September.

Caucasian Yellow (Colias Causasica). Endemic to the Caucasus. Lives in sub-alpine and alpine zones. Very rare.

Hewitson's Black (Erebia Hewitsonii). Caucasus endemic; May to July. Prefers coniferous forests of Lesser Caucasus. Very rare.

Apollo (Parnassiius Apollo) and **Caucasian Apollo.** A mountain butterfly, with some Georgian variations. Found up to 2400 metres. Rare, included in the IUCN Red List.

Beetle

Carabus Caucasicus
A very large, bright blue beetle, up to 5cm with textured back. This dramatic insect-predator is found in deciduous forest up to 2000 metres between April and November (not dangerous).

Photo: David Tarkhnishvili

*For information on Georgia's wildlife see the **Nacres** website at. **www.nacres.org.** Email: administrator@nacres.org*

If you see captive bears in Georgia, please report them to the above email address.

asian Sparrowhawk - 'mimino' in Georgian.

Photo: Zura Javakhishvili

BIRDS

Georgia has over 360 recorded species of bird – and three Caucasus endemic species (seen only here) - the Caucasian Black Grouse, the Caucasian Snowcocks and the Caucasian Chiffchaff. The Caucasus and Cyprus are the only endemic bird areas in Europe – and Georgia is well known as a superb birders destination. The landscape sustains a remarkable variety of habitats for its size and serves as an important migratory and permanent home for many birds. For instance eleven species of eagle and four vultures can be found – particularly around the migratory 'bottle-necks' - mountain passes or Black Sea coast. Several of these are now globally endangered (like the Cinerous Vulture). One can virtually guarantee the sighting of an eagle or vulture in a trip to the mountains, gliding sublimely on thermals – now rare in the Alps and only slightly less in the Pyrenees. Some can be seen quite close-up. I will never forget one autumn evening, standing on a small 2500 metre peak in Tusheti looking *down* on some twenty vultures and eagles spiralling up toward me. The majestic Lammegeier (Bearded Vulture) with its near three metre wing-span is a good goal when in the Greater Caucasus – identified by its size, often reddish breast and more pointed tail. But the southern areas of Georgia are even better for birders than the mountains. They house most of the high-mountain raptors as well as

oto: A Griffon Vulture
des towards Omalo
tress, Tusheti

23

the low-land, cranes, divers, egrets, geese and a great variety of wet-land birds. It's often forgotten that the common pheasant found across Europe and north America, originates from the Caucasian Phasianus Colchicus, named after the Phasis river – former name for today's Rioni river in western Georgia. Now considerably less common in Georgia than in Europe.

Where to see what

THE KAZBEGI REGION is a well known birding venue across Europe, partly due to its relative accessibility, 3 hours north from Tbilisi. The **Lammergeier (Bearded Vulture)** and **Eurasian Griffon Vulture** are common sights along this pathway through the high Caucasus; the

Caucasian Black Grouse

Black **(Cinereous) Vulture** is there in the summer, along with the **Booted Eagle**. The **Golden Eagle** is a permanent resident and you'd be unlucky not to see one if there for more than a couple of days. The showpiece **Caucasian Black Grouse** can be found lurking around the scree, along with the other star the **Caucasian Snowcock**, but require much patience – unless during the Spring when they display. However the dun coloured **Caucasian Chiffchaff** - non-existent outside the region – competes with sparrows for fence posts in the gardens of Kazbegi

Lammegeier

and Gegerti villages. The handsome **Great Rosefinch** is found high up above the tree-line. Its crimson head and breast perching on a rock is a just reward for those taking the

Great Rosefinch

higher walks. But higher up still you might even see **Guldenstadt's Redstart** with its distinctive white cap and rusty belly – it exists nowhere else in Europe. Other less specialist birds you might spot on the way up between the town and the top of the pine woods are – **Corn Crake, Ring Ouzle, Tree and Water Pipits, Redstart, Common Tree Creeper, Wall Creeper, Black Woodpecker, Red-fronted Serin, Eurasian Bullfinch, Twite, Green and Marsh Warblers, Black Redstart, Alpine Swift, Shore Lark, Eurasian Crag Martin, Alpine Accentor, Alpine and Red-billed Choughs, White-winged Snow Finch,**

Caucasian Chiffchaff

Common Crossbill – to name but a few.

THE DAVID GAREJI REGION is a bird paradise (see story on pg 98), with a wider variety of birds than in the high mountains, but less endemic species. Again not far from Tbilisi (1.5 hours south) – but its maximum elevation of 875 metres excludes the more exclusive, high-altitude birds. Having said this – I prefer the David Gareji experience for

Guldenstadt's Redstart

birds. There is less nature-born distraction, the weather is not so changeable and the sparsely treed, flatter valleys make for far easier and longer sightings. Furthermore here is where you encounter the bright coloured feathers, plus more hawks and eagles – and for

Caucasian Snowcock

longer in the year. I hesitate to guarantee sightings of the splendid, white **Egyptian Vulture** with its black wing-tips (especially as it migrates from October and February), but I have never failed in my many visits - furthermore always quite close up, as you spend much of your time around its hunting level, either near the tops of cliffs or on the open plateau roads. **Steppe and Imperial Eagles** and **Black Kites** are often seen in this area, as is the resident **Black (Cinereous) Vulture.** Deviate toward Jandari Lake just to the west and you might see a **White Tailed Eagle** or **Osprey.** En route I often see the brilliant white **Cattle Egrets** prancing aro-

Roller

und animals by the water canals, just south of Rustavi. But for true colours, the Gareji desert plateau and valley is excellent for **European Bee-eaters**, **Rollers**, and occasional **Blue-cheeked Bee-eaters**. Nor must one forget the cheeky and spectacularly crested **Hoopoo** – easily pinpointed by its call (the same as its name). Also seen are - **Peregrine Falcon, Hobby, Saker, Rose-coloured Starling, Rock Thrush, Chukar,**

Bee-eater **Short-toed Snake Eagle, Eurasian Eagle-owl, Long-legged Buzzard, Goshawk, Levant Sparrowhawk, Bimaculated Lark, Rufous-tailed Scrub Robin, Isabelline Wheatear, Finsch's Wheatear, Upcher's Warbler, Eastern Rock Nuthatch, Western Rock Nuthatch, Pale Rock Sparrow, Rock Sparrow.**

Hoopoo

IDENTIFYING

The more common Vultures and Eagles

VULTURES

(wings straight when soaring)

250-295cm	250-295cm	240-280cm	155-180cm

Black (Cinereous) Vulture 'Svavi.'	Lammergeier (Bearded Vulture) 'Batkandzeri.'	Eurasian Griffon Vulture 'Orbi.'	Egyptian Vulture 'Paskunji.'

EAGLES

(wings minutely bent when soaring, tales flatter)

200-240cm	204-220cm	190-210cm

White Tailed Eagle 'Phsovi.'	Golden Eagle 'Mtis artsivi.'	Imperial Eagle 'Begobis artsivi'
174-200cm	145-170cm	100-121cm

Steppe Eagle 'Velis artsivi'	Osprey 'Shaki.'	Booted Eagle 'Chia artsivi.'

© Rafael Antionio Galvez 2005
From: 'Raptors and Owls of Georgia' Buneba Print

All photos © Georgian Centre for the Conservation of Wildlife - GCCW. For more information on Georgia's birds see their website: www.gccw.org

Spring flowers near Mestia, Svaneti

FLORA

Georgia is only 69,700 square kilometres but sustains a remarkable bio-diversity. Subtropical marsh-es, sea coast, semi-deserts, wide alpine pastures and 5000 metres plus peaks – all within a hundred kilometre radius. 40% of its territory is forest – a large proportion of which is classi-fied as genuinely 'virgin.' In addition it has 31 Protected Areas identified for conservation. As a result the country has between 4000 and 4500 species of vascular plants, of which an estimated 15% are endemic to the Caucasus. Of these around 300 are endemic to Georgia alone. Ten species of peony are found, and of the nineteen snow-drop species in the world, Georgia has eight.

Why so many? A million years ago Georgia possessed a tropical climate with accompanying plants. With the last Ice Age, plants that had become extinct in other parts of western Euro-Asia found refuge in the mountain gorges, Colchian lowlands and parts of Eastern Georgia. The subsequent arrivals of frost-resistant plants gradually mingled with the others and evolved together. Consequently many unique species can still be found in this geographically self-contained area – such as the Caucasian rhododendron, Colchian ivy and holly, Imeretian buckthorn and Caucasian species of oak, fir, linden. The Caucasian elm or Water elm (Zelkova carpinifolia) is on the Red Data list. A valuable hardwood not subject to Dutch Elm disease, Georgia still has two main forests, one near Pankisi and one in the Ajameti Reserve near Kutaisi. Like many of Georgia's rare trees, it is protected, but still illegally logged.

Spring is a remarkable time in the Caucasus. Whole mountainsides are carpeted in white, blue and yellow flowers – sometimes inserted with distinctive patches of blood red from Caucasian poppies. While this is found in other mountain ranges, it's rarely with the same degree or diversity. Furthermore in Georgia one can always be sure that nature did the planting.

Iris iberica

Largish white and violet iris (up to 50 cms – flower up to 10 cms) found in dry grasslands up to 700 metres, exclusively in Eastern Georgia. End of March/May. Locally common but increasingly over-picked and sold in markets, so declining. Red Data list species.

Photo: Otar Abdaladze

Papaver ocellatum

(Poppy) – (probably this sub-species) Common Caucasian poppy. 2-4 centimetre petals. Flowers April to June. Plant height 10-40 cms.

Rhododendron caucasium

Evergreen dwarf rhododendron up to 50cm, found between 1600 and 3000 metres covering whole mountainsides. Pale white and also faintly pink flowers – May and July. Rare outside Caucasus.

Galanthus lagodechianus (Snowdrop)

Upper forest, sub alpine zones, 1600-2400 metres, shrub-woods and forest edges. Small flower. Flowers Feb - April.

Fritillaria lutea (Frutillary)
Perennial herb up to 20cm high. Grows in lower alpine zones, meadows. May/June. Considered Caucasian endemic. Quite rare.

Paeonia caucasica (Peony)
Commonest Peony in Georgia. Caucasian endemic. 300-1500 metres. Found in deciduous forests, associated with Oak and Hornbeam forests. Plant up to

a metre, flowers 7cm. April and June.

Rhododendron luteum (Azalia)
Georgia's only deciduous rhododendron. Up to 2 metres. Found in mountains up to sub-alpine zone (around 2200 metres). Gives off rich honey-suckle-like scent that can fill whole valleys (as in Svaneti in June).

Lilium szovitsianum (Lily) ⟶

Powerfully perfumed, spectacular lilly. Found between 400 – 2100 metres, at forest edges; sides of sub-alpine meadows. Large flower-head, plant stands 40-120 cm, flowering June to September. Frequently picked by locals – don't follow their example!

Dactylorhiza urvilleana (Marsh Orchid)
Found in high mountain meadows roughly 1500-2100 metres. Up to 30 cms; flower 10 cms. June/July.

Helleborus caucasicus (Hellebore)
About 20 cms. Found woodlands, roadsides, from sea-level up to 1400 metres,
Feb to April. One of the earliest flowering plants in Georgia. Red Data list. Photo taken in Svaneti.

Tulipa biebersteiniana (small tulip)
Small flower, up to 5 cms. Plant up to 20 cms. Found in dry areas of eastern Georgia up to about 1200 metres, April/May. Red Data species.

Salvia garedji (Clary)
Found in David Gareji steppes. Plant up to 50 cms. Grows in thickets. May to July. Caucasian endemic.

For more academic information on Georgia's flora contact David Kikodze kikodze.david@gol.ge

Photo: Tbilisi's old town – near sto
of Botanical Garden wa

TBILISI

HISTORY

The word 'tbili' means 'warm' in Georgian, and the city of Tbilisi has followed this theme from its earliest beginnings. Developed around its natural hot springs under the 4th century Narikala fortress, the city has offered a warm welcome to travellers ever since; from the traders on the ancient Silk Road to George Bush in 2005. Its reputation for hospitality and exoticism has spread far and wide (I even came across a reference in Oscar Wilde's 'The Portrait of Dorian Grey' of 1891). The domed bath area quickly grew into a focal point for the city. Caravanserais, cafes, churches, mosques, syna-gogues, sprang up. Streets with the names of professions - Silversmith, Blacksmith, Dyer, Wine Hill - radiated out-ward … all still there today. In the early 19th century in its new alliance with Russia, the old town became a haunt for writers and artists. Puskhin, Lermontov, Tolstoy, and as well as Tchaikovsky and Alexander Dumas – all lounged in the sulphurous waters while considering this half-European, half-Asian city and its many nationalities. Within a stone's throw stand the Jewish, Azeri and Armenian quarters - all made up of quaint wood-bal-conied homes. Since then most of the Jews have emigrat-ed to Israel but the Azeris are still there, with mosques and coffee shops to match (as too are the Armenians). Tbilisi old town is unique and will hopefully survive the recent Modernist assault. When the Russians arrived after 1795 - Tbilisi had just been flattened by the Persians - a new architectural style entered the city, the elegant Russian colonial style. Seen particularly along Rustaveli Avenue, but also dotted among the old town. In 1921, after Georgia's brief but intriguing period of independent Menshevik rule, the Bolshoviks arrived and set the scene for the Soviets to begin their 'remodelling by devasta-tion'- as at the base of the old town when constructing the embankment road. Fortunately they stopped there – and more churches survived here than in Russia.

Climbing above the old town on one of the numerous hillside paths (like Walks 1), you quickly see how the city is neatly confined by the Sololaki mountain range to the west and the invisible Tbilisi Sea, to the east. It's easy to observe how the layers of history descended onto the city, and its natural spread outward from the old heart. First, as the grand pre-Revolutionary Russian classical avenues, then the Art Nouveau facades by the old town walls, increasingly dotted with Stalinist creations (like the Parliament on Rustaveli Avenue – an 'idealistically pure' replacement of the beautiful domed Russian cathedral); then finally the Soviet high-rises ringing the city to the east and north. Now Tbilisi enters a new rebuilding stage as the corrupt city planning of the late Shevardnadze period bears fruit and juggernaut apartment blocks rise above rooftops in the Vera and Vake districts like hideous Robo-cops. But now, post Rose Revolution, we trust this era is over…

Walk 1 ══════════

BOTANICAL GARDENS, NARIKALA FORTRESS

Start - Tbilisi Abano area – baths
Finish - Abano or Sololaki regions of Tbilisi
Type - Loop
Date - Al year
Time - 3/4 hours
Upward climb - 350 metres
Max elevation - 700 metres
Grade - Easy
Mobile signal - Permanent

Summary

An excellent means of gathering city bearings and a bird's eye survey of Tbilisi's long and charismatic history (see History Section above). The walk begins in the Azeri/Jewish quarters of the old town, climbs up among the old houses then out onto the promontory of the new Transfiguration Church – to be greeted by the best view in the city. Then comes a long ramble among thinly planted pine forests with occasional startling views. The feel is pure nature, miraculously remote from the city so nearby. After a while the way descends into the tastefully restored Botanical Gardens - a weed and broken glass-strewn ruin until 2002/3, now a haven of waterfalls, terraces, indigenous flowers and shrubs. Exit the garden and step up onto the walls of the Narikala fortress overlooking the whole city and protecting the newly rebuilt St Nicholas Church. Walk on up to the narrow ridge, stand beside the metal skirt of the giant silver Mother Georgia statue (an almost identical copy of the former Soviet one) then descend back, either straight to the Abano district (bath houses) or down into the alleys, balconies, coffee-shops of the quaint Sololaki region of Tbilisi.

Route

The walk starts on the south side of the 'Abano' ('bath house') region at the base of Grishashvili Street. (and might easily end inside one). I like to rendez-vous in one of the Azeri tea-houses on Grishashvili. Glance up and see the goal of the walk's first stage – the new Transfiguration Church perched on a hill almost directly above. Walk up the cobbles to a sort-of T - junction at the top and turn right up Barzovi Street (named after the Georgian Jewish writer). You have now moved into a former Jewish area of Tbilisi (Jews have always been warmly accepted in Georgia). Here the walk turns into a true old-town experience as the road shrinks and eventually seems to dead-end under some washing lines. But look straight ahead and spot stone steps winding on up between the houses. This is the start of the path to the church. Once above the houses the stunning old-town views begin – and continue for much of the walk. Climb up to the church and take in what in my opinion is the best panorama on Tbilisi, then keep walking up behind the monastery buildings to where the access road seems to fork – about 25 metres above the building - and take the path leading away to the right (GPS N 41°41.198: ED44°48 797.817 altitude 510 metres). It leads into some sparsely planted pines which follow the ascending ridge all the way above the Botanical Gardens.

Line up with these two landmarks and then descend from the ridge

'Mother Georgia'

You must follow it too – for nearly an hour. A very pleasant woodland experience, often without path, but with great views of the Botanical Gardens appearing and disappearing through the trees (plenty of birds too). The only tricky moment comes at the top of the walk, spotting the pathway down into the valley behind the Botanical Gardens (GPS N 41°40.770: ED44°47.541 altitude 710 metres). It runs horizontally down the far side of an indentation almost directly opposite the colonnaded restaurant building in front of the TV tower (on the opposite hill – see photo) – or about two hundred metres before levelling with a huge garish villa sticking out of the trees on the nearer opposite hill. From here the walk is downhill all the way (bar one minor moment). If the path (not much used) divides *always* take the downhill option. After about 20 minutes of switchback you come across a larger jeep-track running beside a row

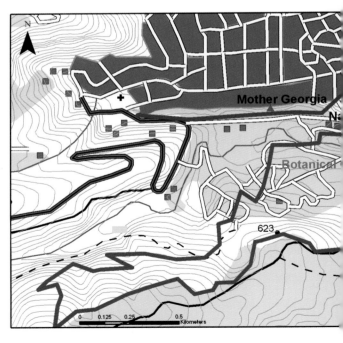

38

of pylons. Follow this down towards Tbilisi, and all the way into the top of the Botanical Gardens (announced by a rusty roofed house poking out of some obviously planted trees) beside a T-junction. Turn right. Once inside the Gardens I offer no directions. Firstly because getting lost in this beautifully restored garden is a joy not a problem; and secondly because by following any downhill direction you will eventually be funnelled toward the exit.

Once outside on the cobbled street, about twenty five metres beyond the gates notice some concrete steps leading left, up to the 4th century Narikala fortress (originally built by the Persians, destroyed a number of times and rebuilt most recently in the post Soviet period, along with its St Nicholas church). Climb to the top, admire more fine views then spot the path running up to the former Comsomol Alley beside which stands the illustrious, silver Kartlis Deda ('Mother Georgia') statue. Many Georgians don't believe that this is in fact an early 1990s replacement of the original Soviet Mother – in a slightly more 'Statue of Liberty' vein. Walk then either straight ahead to the road, following it down into the Sololaki region of Tbilisi *or* head back down to the Fortress then the access road into the old town and the 'abano' region. After this, choose your bath house…

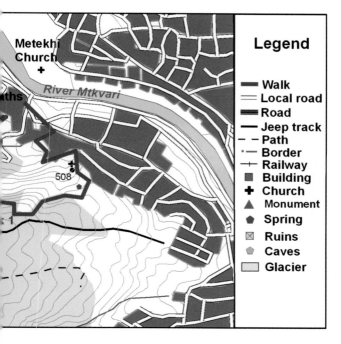

Walk 2 ━━━━━━

SVAN TOWER and ETHNOGRAPHIC PARK

Start/finish - Vake Park entrance (Chachavadze Avenue)
Type - Loop
Date - All year
Time - 2 hours (add an hour for the Ethnographic Park)
Upward climb - 350 metres
Max elevation - 800 metres
Grade - Easy
Mobile signal - Permanent

Summary

An excellent short walk that can, if required, include lunch in one of Tbilisi's most traditional restaurants (Racha), followed by a visit to a large outdoor museum, the Ethnographic Museum. Both are excellent and make this walk good for a Sunday. For the lazy, a cable-car can knock off the initial 200 metre climb (when it works) – up to Turtle Lake – but this will transform the walk into sightseeing. The goal of the walk is visible most of the way – the tall Svanetian tower standing alone on the hill above Turtle Lake. The initial climb toward it is criss-crossed with paths and jeep roads offering numerous variant routes, if the 'straight up' approach offered here seems too much. The walk takes in a number of key Tbilisi landmarks, including Vake Park, formerly the Soviet's Victory Park with its dramatic black, Lady Victory statue lording over the city; the mini-resort, Turtle Lake, with its swimming, boating, and restaurants, the tall Svan tower with stones numbered and carried all the way from Svaneti, then the excellent Ethnographic Museum – with its authentic Georgian wooden homes which many declare as the most 'Georgian' aspect of Georgian architecture. Racha restaurant is one such, found at the upper level of the Park. The food is authentically cooked on a wood stove and served either in wood-walled, windowless room with large fireplace and hung with carpets, or on its spacious balcony with panoramic views across Tbilisi.

NOTE: Several years ago a few muggings were reported in Vake Park and around Turtle Lake. It's better now, but if you want to feel secure, don't do this walk alone.

Route

Walk down the steps into Vake Park from the main entrance on Chavchavadze Avenue and head straight for Lady Victory. You pass fountains, a somewhat non-eternal flame, then face a steep stone staircase straight up to the huge black statue. The Park is dedicated to the Great Patriotic war (WWII) and dominated by this dramatic copper-plated female depicting the cape-flying energy of progress. Although unusually young, with possible Georgian features, she also wields a subliminal threat over the good Soviet citizens – that now the Soviet Union is gone, may be replaced by the male sex. Walk up the long staircase, admire, then keep going straight up into the woods. Using the cable-car lines hanging in the air above as rough guides, choose one of the many paths that continue to pull upward. Keep your eyes peeled for birds – I saw a Hoopoe here a couple of times. Eventually you emerge onto the road to Turtle Lake about a hundred metres from its summit car-park. Refreshment is available – particularly welcome in summer, perhaps even a swim in the small lake's controlled swimming area. Otherwise head on up toward the Svan Tower by taking the upper right hand road leading from the car-park to the cable-car head-station. Two hundred metres on, the jeep-track leads to a

A western Georgian home, in the Ethnographic Park

A Georgian bagpipe player in the Ethnographic Park. The museum's buildings often house tradition craftsmen and the Park occasionally hosts small music festivals.

metal gate, but rather than going through, bear left round the base of the tower's hillock to a second gate. This time pass through it, or the broken fence nearby. Walk up to the tower, take in the view. Attempting entry into the tower is not advised - at the time of writing only a perilous rope hangs from the lower window. Far better to visit the Mestia House Museum in Svaneti itself, than this dislocated emblem of Georgia's most dramatic region.

Down. Walk along the ridge away from the tower (west) then follow the track right, which leads back to the first metal gate encountered on the way up. *Don't go through.* Instead follow the jeep track away to the left. This zigzags down into the top of the architectural park and its first charming wooden houses. Before you know it the cooking smells of Racha restaurant waft into by-now receptive nostrils. The choice is either stop and eat, or continue. Either way don't take the road, but enter the main section of the Architectural Park from behind the restaurant, then walk down and enjoy one of the best collections of regional wooden homes in Georgia – now found less and less, mostly in west Georgia. Be sure to look inside. Leave the Museum park through the main entrance, turn left and walk down the road, switch-back to the right then at the end of the next switch-back bare right onto a jeep track back into the woods. Follow this until you meet the cable-car cables overhead. By now the head of Lady Victory is appearing and disappearing through the trees. Find a suitable path and steer down to her plinth – then down the granite staircase and home into Vake Park.

Dinner Option.

Start later, have dinner rather than lunch at Racha – then call a taxi to take you down from the restaurant (the Museum park may be closed). Better in summer/autumn

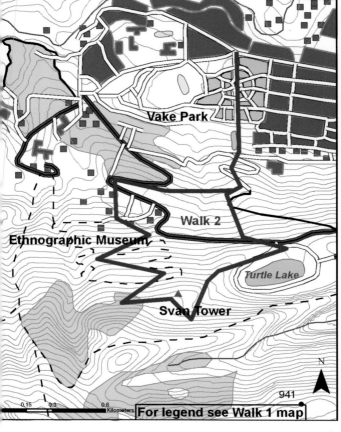

Birtvisi's limestone cliffs from the Goiloli tower. This walk requires some scrambling on all fours. easy to understand Tamurlaine's difficulty capturing the fortress.

BIRTVISI

HISTORY

Built in the 9th century by a local prince, under instructions to create a hidden town, this is a fine example of Georgia's ability to produce medieval fortresses in the most unexpected places. Georgians tell a story about the demise of Birtvisi's seeming impregnability. Tamurlaine's armies had surrounded it for weeks, but the courageous defenders, aided by steep limestone cliffs, repelled all assaults. Finally the exasperated Tamurlaine decided on a cunning ruse. Having observed Georgians closely – he appeared to abandon his attack. His army disappeared, but in fact leaving a few crack climbers at the base of the cliffs. The Georgians, sensing a victory, immediately opened up their kegs of wine and began to celebrate. When drunk and carousing, the troops scaled the steepest of the Birtvisi cliffs, overpowered the gate keepers and signalled for the army to return – which they did and then took the fortress. This story is usually told with an air of pride – as if to imply that the love of a good party may still be exceed the importance of defending impregnable castles.

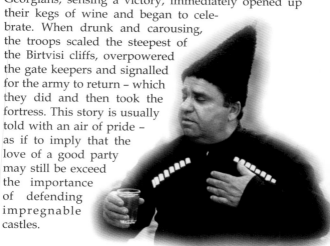

A Kharachorheli musician giving a toast

LOCATION

The Birtvisi fortress is about 1.5 hours south west of Tbilisi – deep in the countryside. Public transport will be difficult – so best to arrange a car/taxi for the day. Take the Marneuli road south out of Tbilisi then, after about 45 minutes turn right just before Koda. Pass through Asureti then just after Partrisi the road forks, *Do not* cross the bridge but keep going straight into Tbisi, located just before an earthen dam. Drive to the top left hand side of the village and park.

BIRTVISI FORTRESS and CANYONS

Start/finish - Tbisi village
Type - One way return with loops
Date - All year
Time - 3/5/6 hours
Upward climb - 350/550/650 metres
Max elevation - 1250 metres
Grade - Walk 3 easy, the others medium/difficult
Mobile signal - Goodish, but is lost down in canyon.

Summary

Three walk options up into the superb canyons around Birtvisi fortress. One of my favourite near-Tbilisi walks into a delightful wooded-canyon. Once inside the shady Caucasian oak forest, vertical cliffs rise up on all sides, some topped with 11th century towers. An hour's climb enables you to look down on forest and this unusual Cappadocian style landscape. Some climbs require all four limbs on hard limestone and creep along near vertical drops – so not for vertigo sufferers. Definitely best in dry weather. Wetness on the rock can make access to the spectacular higher reaches tricky, even dangerous. A guide is recommended if taking on the more complicated fort-summit routes Walks 4 and 5 – although these directions have been tested. The best route is probably 5 – as it goes highest. Walk 3, for non-scramblers, has a couple of steep moments but has been categorised as easy. It still provides fine views.

Routes

All walks begin at the top, left hand end of the village (dam on your left – GPS N 41°35.482: ED44°32.817 Altitude 750 metres). Walk past the last house to the end of the fence then turn right up the hillside (beside the fence). You should soon pick up a strong path (too narrow for jeeps) climbing up the left side of a wooded ridge. It takes you out of the trees, up to a ridge which you follow, even when the path occasionally disappears (it soon returns). Its final section descends through a narrow canyon to the forested main canyon base - a kind of picnic area without tables (about 1.5 hours). I call this place Birtvisi Circus as all routes begin or end here (Walk 3 finishes here). The superb Walks 4 and 5 are more complicated – a local guide is advised (like Sasha, who lives in Tbisi, near the walk start). You have a choice of four directions when standing in the glade at the canyon base (GPS N 41°36.417: ED43°32.262. Altitude 950 metres). A good guide will take you in interesting loops up and down to both fortresses (well worth the small investment). I can only direct you the simplest ways. The trick is finding the starts. Once on the path, they've pretty clear and will lead you all the way to the top - much trod by Georgians from the 11th century onward. Walk 5 Birtvisi Fortress is easier since you can follow the water-course to the left (up) from the Circus base to nearby Arsena's Castle (a small stone tower hugging the canyon wall at GPS N 41°36.366: ED43°32.262). Arsena is Georgia's Robin Hood ('As Saakashvili once saw himself' somebody remarked). Beside it is a spring then the canyon closes down dramatically, sometimes little more than shoulder-width and climbs up and up. Follow this path, it eventually leads out of the canyon, up along a ridge toward the looming massif of the Birtvisi rock towers (about 1.5 hours). The entrance to the fortress is marked by a hole in a crenulated wall. Once inside keep climbing – all the way to the top – the way is steep (sometimes on all fours) but the view is magnificent. We were accompanied by an eager little dog who's tail wagged excitedly at every view point ('a bit like you Peter' as one English friend noted).Walk 4, the Godoli tower (just visible from the Circus through the trees perched on a sheer cliff face 80 metres directly above and to the right) is harder. Essentially straight on from the Circus base (entrance behind you) and then right, winding round the back of the cliff (about 45 minutes). The way is very steep, at times bordering on climbing. Not recommended in the rain.

Down and out – retrace your steps.

Note there are various routes up and down on both Walks (4 and 5) giving the possibility of more interesting loops - but the likelihood of getting lost without a guide is strong. If wanting to explore (I can't advise this), one trick is to climb up first, gain a good view on the wooded Circus area from above, with surrounding rock peaks. If the way is lost, simply climb up above the trees; re-spot the landmarks, and head back down to the Circus – where *hopefully* you will have carefully noted your original way in on Walk 3! Home is to follow it back up to the ridge then down to Tbisi village.

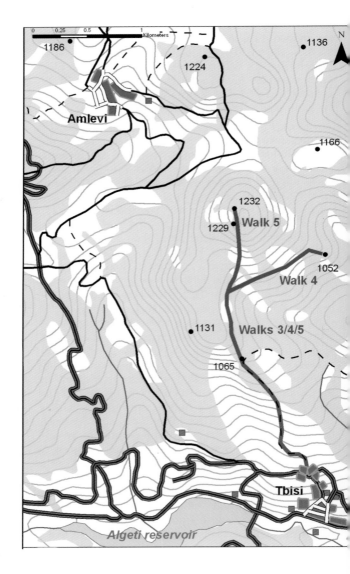

A Georgian warrior from the period of Tamurlaine's invasion, as depicted on the 14th century mural at the Lashtkhveri church in Lengeri, Svaneti.

*The Fire Cross tower - 'Setskhlisjvari koshki' - in lower Gudauri,
destination of Walks 6/7*

GUDAURI REGION

INTRODUCTION and HISTORY

To walk in the Gudauri region is to be in the presence of a great slice of empire-building. Numerous sets of foreign feet have trodden this patch of ground – Pompey and his army (who made it to the 'Gates of Allan' in the Daryal Gorge further up), the Mongols who conquered ruthlessly in the 12th century, the Russians in the 18th and 19th centuries. Until the arrival of air-travel the nearby Jvari 'cross' Pass (2395 metres) served as the main traverse through the high Caucasus. Back in the early 19th century a hundred thousand Russian troops passed through, eyes filled with ambition to take Constantinople back from the Turks (later thwarted by the Communist revolutionaries). Among them the poets Lermontov and Pushkin scanned the white peaks for the Sublime, and gained their first views of the Georgian heartland looking down from atop the Mleta descent on the then new Georgian Military Highway. Today the ski resort of Gudauri offers the same and is currently throwing up new hotels and condominiums with a kind of gold-rush fever. As a result accommodation is rarely a problem. However around this activity (still negligible on European resort standards) are some fabulous walks. Below are just a few.

LOCATION

Gudauri is a 1.5 – 2 hour drive north from Tbilisi, in the Vladikavkaz direction. Quite historic in itself. Arrange transport – or take a taxi. Mini-buses (or marshrutkas) leave from the Didube station ('sadguri') every hour or so – they are marked Kazbegi. Accommodation is plentiful in Gudauri, the Sport Hotel is more expensive but good. Many cheaper, friendly guesthouses surround it, though some close in the summer.

Back. A marshrutka for Tbilisi leaves every afternoon from the Gudauri Sport Hotel car park – ring the hotel to check times.

Walks 6/7 ━━━━━━━━━

The FIRE CROSS TOWER

Start/finish - Gudauri Sport Hotel in lower Gudauri
Type - Loop
Date - May - October
Time - 3 or 4 hours.
Upward climb - 200 or 400 metres
Max elevation - 2200 or 2400 metres
Grade - Easy/moderate, both walks
Mobile signal - More or less permanent

Summary

Two very similar and easy walks from the Gudauri Sport Hotel complex and back, in a circle. After about twenty minutes you encounter a feisty, but not enormous climb up onto a ridge with splendid views down into the historic Khada Gorge – former route of the Military Highway with a reputed 60 towers (not all standing). The walk can be various lengths. If you are fresh arrivals at 2000 metres (the hotel's starting altitude) and concerned about fitness, you may want to take the easy route (Walk 6), which involves just one steepish climb – up to the first ridge. From that moment everything is more or less flat or downhill – save for a short climb right at the end. The overall distance is short and it's very hard to get lost once up on the ridge as the whole walk becomes visible. If at times a main path disappears – this is of less concern in the Caucasus where the idea of private property in open countryside is less possessive than in Europe. Just head toward your goal. The only threat is dogs but here are usually only aggressive close to homes or sheep (the walk avoids homesteads). Walk 7 is the same but with an add-on ridge climb mid-way.

Route

Head out the back of the Gudauri Sport Hotel towards the chair lifts. Walk down past the embarkation point then on under the hanging chairs along a jeep track. Follow this round and up a small hillock to the right, then just beyond this a track branches away to the left. Shortly thereafter you encounter what used to be a small crater lake, but now overgrown with reeds. Follow the rim

52

round to a path heading for a gully that climbs gently up to a grassy valley – at which point it loses definition. But don't worry – your route is now simple - up and to the right. The next immediate goal is the ridge at the summit of this hill. You can just make out a path near the top. (For an easier but longer route head straight up the valley then join the path and back-track to the right). The top looks far but isn't - and how you get up is entirely your choice – straight or zig-zag. As soon as you reach the crest the entire walk becomes clear. You can see the 12th century Fire Cross tower ('Setskhlisjvari koshki') - cutting against the sky straight ahead, and a path tacking across the hillside towards it. Behind you stands the now diminutive Sport Hotel; ahead and below are pastures and the edge of Setorebi hamlet. The 'easy' route referred to in the Summary, is to follow this path, tacking along the side of the mountainside to the tower (Walk 6).

The less easy route (Walk 7) - which I prefer, then keeps climbing the ridge rising up to the left - for another kilometre. This takes you to altitudes 2400 plus metres, granting a corresponding improvement of view - especially of the Khada Gorge. You end up at the junction of two ridges, one leading straight to the Fire Cross tower, now some way below. You then have to walk down this fairly steep ridge toward it. But as it neatly intersects both valleys the view is magnificent. You see the full length of the chair lift – and even have an option of changing walks and heading on up to the cable-car mid-station and 'Kosta's hut' at 2700 metres (a stiff climb).

Assuming you don't – you arrive at the Fire Cross tower, one of the rarer rounded towers of the Caucasus (most are square). After looking round head back to the nearby neck of the ridge then turn downhill, steeply to the left. There is a sort-of path straight down into the pastures. Once it starts to level off, continue in the same direction across the fields then across a small burn in a gully. On the other side, cross a field to pick up a jeep track heading left toward the Seturebi hamlet. Take it but avoid the houses by following the road around the base of the hill to the right. The path leads up a short spur after which the Sport Hotel is visible again, slightly above and ahead. The way is then clear. It's more pleasant to stay off the main road and head through the field of gas pipeline pressure valves - Georgia's vital gas supply from Russia, toward the Sport Hotel's rear entrance by the chair lift base station.

Walk 8 ═══════

<u>LOMISA CHURCH</u>

Start/finish - Mleta village
Type - loop
Date - May - October
Time - 4/5 hours
Upward climb - 800 metres
Max elevation - 2400 metres
Grade - Moderate
Mobile signal - Permanent

<u>Summary</u>

This small. spireless church is visible from just about everywhere in the Gudauri region. It sits atop the Lomisa ridge like a matchbox breaking the skyline. The view from the top is stunning – as it is all the way up. The church is also one of the oldest in Georgia – built in the 9th century on a famous pagan site. Later a monastery was added and amazingly the frontispiece still stands just over the ridge top – like a mini Georgian Tintern Abbey. Considering the date and location - at some 2200 metres on an exposed ridge – the significance of this place cannot be underestimated. Every year, on 'Wednesday in the seventh week after Pentecost,' (so close to the summer solstice it can hardly be a coincidence) several thousand people from the Mtiuleti, Khevi and Khevsureti districts make a pilgrimage up to this church to celebrate Lomisoba. Inside a heavy chain lies next to the church's central pillar. Devotees must lift the chain, place it round their neck and walk (or better crawl) round the pillar three times anti-clockwise - making a wish (usually, apparently, to be married). It's been done for centuries. As to the chain's origins – rumours abound. Some even say it's a descendent from the chain that held Amirani (the Georgian Prometheus) to the massif of Mt Kazbek (the two myths have curious parallels - see page 75). Just over half way up the 700 metre climb stands a small stone 'salotsavi' ('holy place'), adorned with candles – not unlike those found in pagan Khevsureti and Tusheti, except with a cross on top. The walk from the bottom is a good two hour climb. The way down follows the adjacent ridge to make a small loop. Once on top it's

The monastery just over th
ridge beside Lomisa chur

hard to resist some ridge-walking off to the right toward Lomisa peak – which can raise the altitude to 2400+ metres. The ridge can be followed for virtually any distance, but on this walk only amounts to an hour's diversion on top of the world. The adventurous may try to extend the ridge walk into a full day trip – by descending a couple kilometres higher up the Aragvi valley. But this is untested – and not part of this walk.

NOTE: Those taking mini-buses from Tbilisi should get off (and on again) at Mleta. Be prepared to wait on the return as sometimes they're full.

MYTHOLOGY

According to legend the Ottomans invaded this region and carted 7000 prisoners back to northern Turkey as slaves. However these slaves bought nothing but bad luck and failed crops, so the Turks tried to destroy their precious talisman, the icon of St George. However rather than melting, the icon miraculously attached itself to the horns of a bull called 'Loma' (the Georgian for 'lion'). After this miracle the Georgians were allowed to let this magical bull lead them back to their homeland. On arrival he climbed up to the site of the Lomisa church and died. The monastery was then built in homage. Hardly could there be a more thorough blending of Christian and pre-Christian mythologies...

View towards the Lomisa ridge from the top of the Aragvi gorge, on Walk

Route

M leta village sits beside the Aragvi river, just across the bridge at the bottom of the switchback climb up to Gudauri. Organise a lift down – takes about ten minutes - and arrange a rough time for the lift back. Here mobile phones come into their own – reception is good on the entire walk. The way up starts at the lower end of Mleta village, away from the bridge, near the blue and white police checkpoint. Just before and on the opposite side of the road a jeep track heads up to the right. Walk up about 75 metres past the school to where the path divides. 20 metres up a small path leads left between allotments (GPS N 42°25.673: ED44°30.627 Altitude 1490 metres). This is the beginning of the walk and winds away up the hill into the open pastures above the village. By now the path is very clear and a wood approaches. The pilgrim's way steers up and in with a steep right hand turn – then switch-backs up through the trees. After a period of stiff climbing the path emerges above the trees and the view opens up. Keep going and soon a small plateau appears with a stone cross 'salotsavi' standing in the centre. The way is pretty obvious – on and up – the church is now clearly visible on the ridge directly above with its out-of-character new roof. As you close in on the top the valley to the right merges with the mountainside. Take note of a path dividing off from yours to head down along its ridge – this is the way down (making the loop).

At the top step into the strangely Tardis-like Lomisi church (larger than it seems from the outside). Partly buried under the ridge this is a heroic, ancient structure (called Lomisi by locals) – in a fantastically exposed position. Inside the roof is supported by a single pillar. A heavy chain lies at its base – and men will lift the chain, drape it round their neck then walk round the pillar in an anticlockwise direction three times. Outside the church entrance a second large river valley opens up – and even more surprisingly right before it stands the remains of a large stone portico – former entrance to the monastery. The arch and two ragged columns remain but stand a good ten metres high up on that wind-and snow- blasted ridge – in a kind of miracle of church-survival.

To the right the splendid ridge winds its way north west. Follow it for as long as you please (I suggest half an hour out and half back). Mt Lomisa will add another 250 metres to the walk, is very steep and requires a further half hour at least. The peaks can be avoided by cutting them off and walking below. But of course you miss the double-sided views.

Back. Retrace your steps to the Lomisi church, then start down the path toward Mleta, but about 100m below the top branch off to the left where the path divides at the head of the valley. Follow this narrower left hand ridge path all the way down to the village to make the loop – the way is obvious and mostly ridge-top. The bottom is quite steep but manageable. It returns you to the other end of Mleta village, near its upper bridge (a possible rendez-vous point for your lift).

upper part of Mleta village as seen from the Georgian Military Highway

57

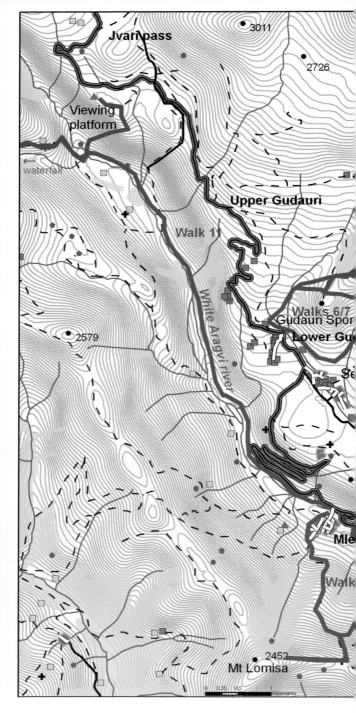

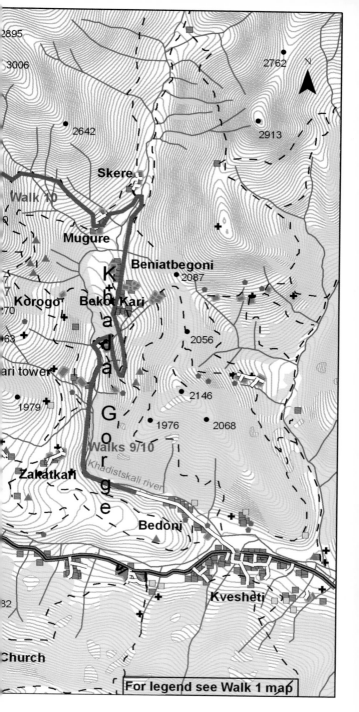

For legend see Walk 1 map

APOCALYPSE BROW

We arranged for a lift down from the Gudauri Sport hotel to Mleta, the village directly. The lift was a synch compared to the one to Khada the previous day, when our new 'friend' from the guest house said he'd arrange everything for 40 lari. When it came time to pay it changed to 40 lari per person. The Academy Award set of wide eyes accompanying the, 'what didn't you understand? almost made it worth the 160 lari hike. Needless to say he accepted the protested 60 we gave him. While driving down the switchback I tried to spot the route up to the church. Everybody we asked beforehand knew the way, had said 'yes very easy, no problem, can't miss the path,,,' but none could give that crucial information – where did it start? All we could get was 'Mleta.' There seemed two possible routes - along two small valley shoulders rising up on either side of the village. The entire mountainside leading to the church was visible so I scoured it for any sudden gorges or landslides blocking the way. Both seemed clear, but the left hand route seemed wider - so we had ourselves dropped at the blue and white former police station. When I looked around it quickly became obvious - time for the old Moscow Airport technique (developed during the chaotic post-Soviet period) 'when in doubt follow the largest group of people.' Nearby a couple of children headed up a track toward the school. So that was it. After a quick consultation with an old woman – the technique proved infallible again. Soon we were striding up the wide pilgrim's way – through steep green pastures then switch-backing through pleasant oak woodland. After about an hour the path opened up on a flat plateau displaying absolute confirmation of the correct route – a small stone cross bedecked with burnt-out candles. Standing beside it looking out across the valley I tried to picture the scene some two months earlier; some 2000 pilgrims swarming round, lighting candles, pronouncing prayers on the way up to the small chapel on the ridge above.

As we climbed I mentioned to my companion I'd saved a couple pieces of Khachapuri (Georgian cheese bread) for lunch at the top – since this was Georgia and there'd be no cute cappuccino kiosk by the church. We'll be 'gloriously alone with the view.' Shortly after saying this I noticed a large Russian MI8 helicopter wopping steadily across the valley heading, it seemed, straight for the church. Surely not! But as if invited by my words, it touched down right next to it. Outrageous! Flying to the one place which we pilgrims struggled… I remembered someone mentioning a political convention at the Gudauri Sport Hotel. Probably some politicians too lazy to walk - shame! Meanwhile the helicopter completed a neat landing on a small patch of grass, its tail dangling dramatically over the ridge, then after a few minutes lifted off again, only to return. Odd… politicians would require just one trip there and back. Perhaps the military – setting up an observer station on Ossetia just a few kilometres away beyond the ridge (then during one of the political flare-ups)? I could see a bold white and red Georgian flag near the church – a message to the Ossetians? I struggled to see if any of the figures stepping out wore uniforms – but all silhouetted black against the sky. Perhaps not army engineers but priests re-supplying the church – the Georgian church was increasingly wealthy; but enough to hire a helicopter for a whole day….?

In truth I was baffled.

Forty five minutes later we arrived at 2200 metres beside the small stone church – now swarming with over 50 people, some carrying stones and cement. Ahead, just over the ridge, stood the bizarre ruins of a small monastery; about half of its front portico still standing, waiting it seemed for that final puff of wind to bring it crashing to the ground, Beside it stood a man stirring a boiling vat of mutton soup. He beckoned at us furiously, then filled two glasses to the brim from a dirty Fanta bottle. He stretched out his arms as everyone looked on grinning. 'Welcome,,, drink!' he shouted. The liquid was slightly opaque, odourless, possibly a kind of rose wine. But whatever it was, we'd no choice. Down it went… with suitable nods of gratitude. But in fact not too bad – a light home-made wine, except that what we really craved after our climb was water. 'Tskhali?' I tried to pronounce this notoriously difficult Georgian word for 'water.' The grinning faces merely grinned on and the glasses were re-filled. But years in Georgia had prepared me. Rather than taking the glasses, I walked around looking through various buckets and bottles until finding something that resembled drinking-water. I found a cup and dipped it in. 'OK?' I inquired, hoping that if it was something lethal they'd tell me. 'OK!' came a reply and quickly they got the drift. Other glasses were found and we had our fill of spring water and hunks of a delicious goats cheese – then we downed the final toast, acknowledging our 'friend-ship' (see glossary).

After this the mystery slowly unfolded. It seemed a young 'New Georgian,' had hired the helicop-ter for the day to help restore this revered church. A smiling, slightly podgy man of about 30 whose occu-pation I could only discover was 'business,' because a far more inter-esting topic loomed - 'the supra' (Georgian feast) to imminently follow the work's comple-tion. 'You are coming!' we were told emphatically. I glanced at the angle of the sun. Supras went on and on. We had a two hour walk home and per-haps three hours of daylight. But my English companion was keen – this was his first week in Georgia. And something told me the helicopter pilot wouldn't desert their foreign guests. I asked to meet him, and a few minutes later up stepped the famous Shamil from Tusheti, one of Georgia's top pilots. We knew each other vaguely from precious trips up to his remote home in the north-eastern corner of Georgia - accessible eight months of the year only by helicopter. I noticed with, I confess, some re-assurance, he now wore a pistol strapped to his hips. So, with return jour-ney assured we completed our walk up the ridge and down. The workers finished their repairs to Lomisa's entrance then stepped inside to carry the chain around the pillar three times. When we returned the supra was already underway on a long low table in the lee of the church. Details then become hazy, but I do remember my English companion repeatedly draining his glass 'bolomde' ('to the bottom') and Shamil's final toast. Holding his glass up in the slanting light, he acknowledging this beautiful place, the church and in a wave of the glass, all of Georgia. Suddenly I could feel it there with us, its peaks, valleys and churches spreading out like a coloured tourist map from this ridge top. Finally as the sun set, the turbines roared and a lurching group hurried toward the helicopter. Climbing on board my friend shouted that this was his first ever helicopter ride. 'And your last,' I shouted back. Seconds later it lifted off, soared into an 'Apocalypse Now' 90-degree turn then dived down into the valley. But did we care if we lived or died? For had we not been fully captured by the spirit of these wild mountains, now literally lifting us from the ground and hurling our bodies through the air towards the rapidly approaching Gudauri Sport Hotel. Four minutes later we stood, incredulous, back on terra firma, watching Shamil wheel the helicopter up into the air for the final worker's shuttle. As the moon rose up behind the Fire Cross tower our fellow passengers called us to yet another supra – but I dragged my companion unwillingly away. We had started the day as pilgrims, ended it as virtual alcoholics, then briefly soared through the night sky under a burning full moon. The Caucasus had provided what it so often does – the totally unexpected - and we'd survived. Enough!

The KHADA GORGE

Start - Bedoni village (turn off at Kvesheti and cross river)
Finish - Bedoni village (Walk 9). Gudauri Sport Hotel (Walk 10)
Type - One way return (Walk 9). Single direction (Walk 10)
Date - May – November (Walk 9). May – October (Walk 10)
Time - 4/5 hours and 6/7 hours
Upward climb - 300 metres and 900 metres
Max elevation - 1800 metres and 2400 metres
Grade - Easy (Walk 9). Moderate (Walk 10)
Mobile signal - Surprisingly good except at valley end.

Lower section of the Khada gorge, near Bedoni village

HISTORY

Once while staying in Gudauri I heard someone remark about a fellow worker; 'Oh he's from Khada, he's OK.' On further questioning it seemed that people from this valley had a reputation - for being calmer, more self-contained, less prone to the excesses of the Mokhebi (those from Kazbegi region). Was it, I wondered, due to the antiquity of this valley: its reported beauty? Containing a rumoured 60 stone towers and several villages, its communities had developed alongside the main route through the Greater Caucasus before the Russians built the Georgian Military Highway up the steep Mleta cliffs in the early 19th century. Here the huge mountain barrier is at its narrowest – a mere 60 kms (unlike the 120km around Svaneti). With the new road, this valley had suddenly found itself retired from the bustle of armies, Silk Road travellers, diplomats etc and had settled back into more agrarian ways.

Summary

This walks up through a historic mountain gorge that then opens into a spacious, tower-dotted valley with a remote, high-alpine atmosphere – yet only one and a half hours drive from Tbilisi. The reported 60 towers are not all standing, but Khada's several upper villages are permanently inhabited. To reach them the road follows the Khadistskali river gorge with villages perching like eagle's nests on top of vertical cliffs. The gorge is long (10 kilometres just on the road – which requires a jeep save at the start) but because of its dramatic beginnings, worth making the effort to walk most of it. The longer walk (Walk 10) ends with a steep 600 metre climb up to the ridge above the Gudauri Sport Hotel. From there it's a pleasant one hour down - straight to the hotel bar. However that final two hour climb gives the tale a fairly sharp sting. For those with shorter time (and breath) it's also possible just to walk the gorge up to the higher villages and back (Walk 9). This will still take a good four hours and is an excellent walk.

NOTE: For those relying on marshrutkas (mini-buses) – you can start and end the walk at Kvesheti village on the main Tbilisi road, but add an hour.

Route

The official beginning of the gorge is Bedoni village. It stands beside the White Aragvi river at the gorge entrance about three kilometres down toward Tbilisi from Mleta. Turn off at Kvesheti village (about 15 minutes by car from the Gudauri Sport Hotel). Cross the Aragvi and drive the jeep track under the gas pipe and through the first village – Bedoni (this could easily be walked but lengthens the walk). Once on the other side (away from all potential dog trouble) this is a good place to be dropped. Ahead, giant cliffs rise up like a Hollywood set, and built-into one of the first is a small prison - originally for North Caucasian invaders. The walk just takes the jeep track all the way up to the top village (Skere) (about 7 more kms) – so its neigh-on impossible to get lost. The road climbs slowly and steadily and soon gives views of Zakatkari and Korogo villages perched like eeries above massive cliffs. Hard not to imagine elves up there. Now begins a long-running mystery as to the way up. At this point the road follows the right hand side of the valley, while the village is high up on the left. The mystery was only solved up at Bekot Kari village – by an old woman who pointed back down the valley saying, by 'khidi' (bridge). This obviously raised the possibility of a second walk up the Khada gorge – on the left hand side (not yet tried). Locals later also alluded to this – hinting at a shorter route back to the Gudauri Sport Hotel. But this misses out the delightful higher pastures and villages, as well as the picturesque Church of St George and bell tower at Bekot Kari. Inside the churchyard we spotted a new gravestone carved with two faces, one with dates, one without. Here Walk 9 ends (although in truth it can be continued up the valley as far as you want)

Walk 10. After the church keep going along the road toward the final village – Skere. Cross the bridge but before Skere turn left to Mugure, the next village back on the left side of the valley. The climb up to the ridge starts directly above this village. Shortly after the first dwellings appear look for a path leading up the hill to the right – but larger than one for a specific house. This will be the main path that leads eventually up over the pass. You should find yourself tracking back up the valley but above the village climbing along the side of a small valley shoulder. Soon you gain its ridge which must be followed until just short of the moment it meets with the main valley flanks. Here the path mysteriously divides – with a smaller track leading downward slightly to the left. The main path continues straight along the ridge then appears to bank left along the valley flank. *Do not follow it.* Instead take the smaller left hand track. If you follow the main (and former path) you will eventually be halted by a large new landslide – and have to back track a good ten minutes. The smaller path takes you down slightly into the crook of a small valley, across the dividing stream then up the steep final flanks to the pass. This last bit is further than it looks and climbs up to 2400m so prepare for a good puff. The top is marked by a shepherd's hut and a view of the Gudauri Sport Hotel nestling down below at the base of a long shallow valley. Directly above is the head station of the second cable car and 'Kosta's hut and restaurant' – manned 'sometimes' during summer months. Ahead are two paths – upper and lower – following the general direction of the Gudauri Sport Hotel (left and down). The upper seems tempting – as it seems to offer a regain of the ridge at a higher elevation (hence longer views) – but it soon vanishes, as the cows (its obvious creators) fanned out to pasture. The lower path is the genuine route and picks up the ridge at a lower level (with views down into the Khada Valley). It also divides later on offering a quick way home (right hand route) by avoiding the ridge altogether and following the valley down to its apex, where all three routes down must converge (GPS N 42°27.968: ED44°29.487 Altitude 2060 metres). Here a narrow path runs along the right side of a gully to a small plateau dominated by a former lake. Follow the rim round the left hand side of the lake then pick up the jeep track to the hotel at the base of the chair lift (GPS N 42°27.760: ED44°29.096 Altitude 2005 metres).

Gravestone in Bekot Kari

Walk 11 ═══════

<u>ARAGVI GORGE and WATERFALL</u>

Start - Soviet Viewing Platform – 2 kms beyond Upper Gudauri
Finish - Mleta
Type - One way - mostly downhill (sometimes steep)
Date - May - October
Time - 5/6 hours
Upward climb - 200 metres (down 900 metres)
Max elevation - 2275 metres
Grade - Medium, bar a few scrambling moments at top
Mobile signal - Amazingly good, save in upper valley.

Summary

A dramatic walk – starting at its highest point to descend into the upper Aragvi valley – then, bridges permitting, up towards an elegant waterfall. The walk could also be done in reverse by those liking to finish high - leaving the steepest climb and finest views for the end (add an hour). However this is less advisable post mid-September as the valley's splendid view is cut in half by afternoon shadows. The initial descent has a couple of scrambling moments down an, at times, heavily overgrown path – but nothing outdoing a modicum of common sense. Furthermore the way is pretty logical – I managed to find it alone (my guide had 'a knee incident' returning from the bar the night before). There is one river to cross at the bottom of the valley – I had to effect a temporary bridge repair. But the pastures beyond are much used by cattle so I suspect bridges re-appear each spring. If it's gone – then the river is easy (shallow) to wade (at least from mid August). If it seems too tricky all is not lost – you simply skip the waterfall and walk on down this splendid valley gorge, past the ruins of stone villages, hanging cliffs, to Mleta. Remember you need a lift back up to Gudauri (if staying there), unless you want to add a couple more hours of road-walking at the end.
NOTE: The drop offs could be made by marshrutka (mini-bus). Descend at the Viewing Plaform, do the walk, then get on again at Mleta in the afternoon. If you want to make this walk in one day from Tbilisi, you'd need to start very early.

Head of the Aragvi valley, looking south

Route

Have yourselves dropped at the Soviet Viewing Platform. This is the ugly, circular mosaic illustrating the 'friendship' between the Georgian and Russian peoples, perched at the edge of the Aragvi gorge, about 150 metres below the top of the Jvari pass (1 km after the avalanche tunnel). Unmissable in its bizarreness – as a viewing platform that blocks the view (with Soviet propaganda). The start of this walk is more critical than most. You must find the spot where the path summits onto the Viewing Platform plateau at (GPS N 42°29.353: ED44°27.486 Altitude 2250 metres). Without electronics, face the Viewing Platform from the approach-road and head left. There's a faint path aiming in a straight line toward the last house across the gorge in upper Gudauri. Follow this sight-line through a couple of semi-bogs to the eastern edge of the plateau and look down. (If you arrive at the cross cairn – you're too far right, follow the eastern plateau flank to the left). You should spot the path about 25 metres down from the top, about mid-way along the plateau. Once found the way is obvious (the drop is very steep below) and soon leads to a stunning view-point up and down the Aragvi valley (including the waterfall). Descent to the Aragvi river is about one hour. Arrival is marked by a distinctive solitary memorial stone carved almost life-size in the form of a man wearing a chokha (traditional Caucasian dress with cartridge holders). Cross the nearest river (two merge just below) and head up the opposite valley flanks to the ruined stone hamlet at the top. You can see the waterfall over to the west and the path is obvious. Stay on the top, don't attempt to climb down to the waterfall's foot. View it from the cliff-top directly ahead, then retrace your steps back to the river. Beyond it is a distinctive jeep track that heads all the way down to Mleta.

NOTE: Rising up in the middle of the Aragvi valley is a small hillock topped by another ruined village. You can visit this by crossing the second river (a small bridge existed when I walked this, but had disappeared by the time of writing), but be aware that you'll have to retrace your steps back to this bridge to cross back to the main Mleta jeep track (unless another bridge has since appeared below).

ue at the bottom of
White Aragvi gorge

The **KAZBEGI REGION**

INTRODUCTION

The Kazbegi region attracts more walkers than any Georgian destination. At only three hours drive from Tbilisi - up the historic Georgian Military Highway - the town sits under the 5033 metre Mt Kazbek. Furthermore it is overlooked by the 14th century Sameba church perched on a hilltop 400 metres directly above the village of Gerteti. In the evening the church and bell-tower silhouette against Kazbek's eternal snows to create one of Georgia's more enduring images. Walks abound here – of every level, complexion and drama. From the flat, geologically intense Truso valley, to the venerated climber's approach to Mt Kazbek itself, up to the dazzling Gergeti glacier at 3100 metres. In the Kazbek region one senses the enormous geological forces that gave Georgia its dramatic landscape, and also, by proxy, its people their character. Four separate walking areas are presented here – using Kazbegi as base. Three require drop-offs and pick-ups afterwards, one (the first) can be walked from the town - or Gergeti (its neighbour just the other side of the Terek river -Tergki in Georgian).

Mt Kazbek and the Sameba church

LOCATION

Kazbegi is a small town of about three thousand, due north of Tbilisi, about three to three and a half hours by car (35 minutes by helicopter). The region is called Khevi and the people who inhabit it, Mokheve. It has a good marshrutka (mini-bus) service, departing from Tbilisi's Didube sadguri ('station'), but a car is best - I like to choose a sturdy looking taxi at a rank. They can be shared for only slightly more than the marshrutka cost – and stopped for photos/sightseeing at places like Ananuri by the Zhinvali reservoir. You also pass through Gudauri (another walking centre) and some people stop off. Taxis from Kazbegi are also available back – some driven by Formula 3 champions (I once did the three hour plus journey in 2 hours and five minutes – sweating more than on the Kazbek hike). Kazbegi has one comfortable hotel, Stephantsminda, and numerous guest-houses/homestays (like Vano's in Gergeti or the Kazalikashvilis in Kazbegi– ask in the town square for directions). The central square is a taxi centre for trips, either up to the Gergeti church, or for the various walks offered here.

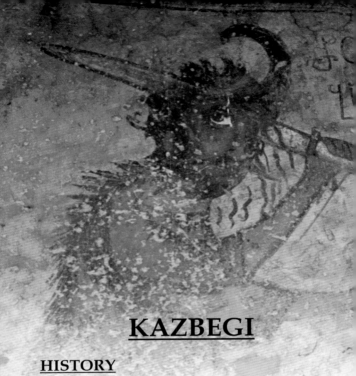

<u>KAZBEGI</u>

<u>HISTORY</u>

The names Kazbek and Terek (Kazbegi's river) stem from Mongol roots – imposed on this, then tiny settlement during the Mongol invasion of the 12th century. They stuck. After Mongol influence faded, Georgian Orthodoxy re-asserted its presence on this crucial, northern border-marker of Georgia, by building the spectacular Sameba church directly under Mt Kazbek, in the 14th century – a time when churches not maps marked out territories. Georgians have their own name for Mt Kazbek (an extinct volcano), which is Mkinvartsveri ('top of glacier'). They also have their own name for Kazbegi – Stephantsminda - but a local poet Alexander Kazbegi, a kind of Mokheve Walter Scott, renamed it in the 19th century. There is an interesting museum dedicated to him in the town centre, beside the Armenian style church – with old photographs of many of the towers encountered on these walks (note the alarming rate of decay). Kazbegi also sits at the head of the famous Daryal Gorge, celebrated by Russia's romantic 19th century poets (see Walk 18). For more information on the mountain itself (although mostly untranslated) a small Museum of Alpinism waits neglectedly for visitors on the first parallel street above the town centre, opposite the Kazalikishvili's house.

MYTHOLOGY

Many stories lie buried within the fallen stones of these mountain villages. I like asking locals to recite any they know (it helps keep them alive). The Amirani myth is one such. It comes in many forms, some showing similarities with the Greek myth of Prometheus. Both demi-gods were chained to Mt Kazbek as punishment. Prometheus stole fire for human-kind, but Amirani, after a fest of super-human feats and dragon-slayings, decided to challenge God to a contest. After all his warnings went unheeded, God threw his staff into the ground and asked Amirani to pull it out. Amirani tried but of course failed because the stick had grown roots deep into the earth. For his foolishness he was chained to the mountain and a raven sent to feed him bread and wine every day. For a fuller rendition see the book 'Georgia, in the Mountains of Poetry' (I'm afraid by me...). To see a powerful 14th century mural illustrating part of the Amirani myth, visit the Lashtkhveri church in Lengeri, near Mestia in Svaneti,

The photo above is a section of this mural

Walks 12/13 ═══════════

SAMEBA CHURCH and GERGETI GLACIER

Start/finish - Kazbegi or Gergeti villages
Type - One way return with possible loops
Dates - May – Dec (Walk 12). May – Oct (Walk 13) snow allowing
Time - 2 hours and 7/8 hours
Upward climb - 400 metres and 1300 metres
Max elevation - 2210 metres and 3100 metres
Grade - Easy (Walk 12). Medium but strenuous (Walk 13)
Mobile signal - Permanent (Walk 12). Permanent to 2950 metres, then none (Walk 13)

Summary

The two classic walks of Georgia's mountains, done more frequently than any others. The first takes you up to the 14th century Sameba (Trinity) church, bell-tower and small monastery overlooking Kazbegi village. The second continues on up another 1000 metres toward the summit of Mt Kazbek (but stops, two days climb short) on a dramatic cliff overlooking the ice-sheet of the Gergeti glacier. One of the two is nigh-on essential to any visit to Georgia. On the second you pick up the footsteps of Douglas Freshfield, of the London Alpine Club, who first climbed Mt Kazbek in 1868 and later became Director of the Royal Geographic Society and wrote his 2-volume, 'The Exploration of the Caucasus.' Today climbing Mt Kazbek typically involves a four-day expedition. To do so, consult the 'Finding a Guide' section on page 10.

Route

Walk 12 - to Sameba Church. Walk (from Kazbegi) down to the river, across the Terek bridge (Tergi in Georgian) then immediately left up the road to the top of Gergeti village. At the T junction you have three choices, all lead to the church, **Left** takes you up via the small ruined watch-tower to the left of the hill. Enter the gully by the tower, continue along the stream then take one of the several paths *up* (to the right). Eventually you see the church in open pastures above. **Right** merely follows the jeep

Door to the Same
chur

track all the way to the top (the slowest, easiest route). **Straight-on** actually begins about 20 metres to the right, where you turn left up a small track among the houses (GPS N 42°39 787: ED44°37.798 Altitude 1850 metres), then at the next street, straight-on again along another track which eventually leads above the houses. Keep climbing past a small cemetery along by open grass pastures to a wood, then up through the trees until eventually regaining the road. Follow it round to the plateau and open pastures to the church (GPS N 42°39.735: ED44°37.213 Altitude 2210 metres).

Walk 13, to the Gergeti glacier starts just beyond the point where the road to the church crests the hill (GPS N 42° 39 931: ED44°36 868 Altitude 2180 metres). You can see the way clearly – up along the ridge to the right. A fabulous walk. On a good day Mt Kazbek stays with you all the way and the ridge opens up on a deep valley with multicoloured rocks and trees (in the autumn). Meanwhile the ridge soars you up into the sky, shrinking the Sameba church into two small dots and revealing more and more of the surrounding peaks. There is another way, a more well-trod 'climbers route' which avoids the sometimes blustery ridge top (and Kazbek views). About 200 metres along the first stretch of ridge-top a path leads away to the left, along the left hand flank of the hillside (GPS N 42°39 980: ED44°36.441 Altitude 2320 metres). Said to be slightly easier, it parallels the ridge route lower down, all the way to the top where both paths meet beside the 'salotsave' (holy place) - a large cairn of stones, sometimes decorated with candles

and/or crosses (GPS N 42°39 521: ED44°34.402 Altitude 2960 metres). A place of amazing panoramas and a suitable reward for all the panting. Be aware that by now altitude is a factor. People feeling slightly dizzy or strangely tired shouldn't push themselves. Take frequent rests, drink lots of water (plenty of clean water lies in the streams ahead – now safely above the summer pastures). From this point on the high mountain moraine begins; the Gergeti glacier clearly visible immediately below the Kazbek massif. Its drastic ice-shrinkage is marked out by two giant, empty cliffs of red rock opening out below the tongue. The destination of the walk is on top of the left hand cliff, just above the end of the tongue. The path from the salotsavi leads straight to it – and is well marked by climber's cairns. On our trip heavy cloud and snow suddenly descended some forty minutes on, just below the snow bucket (a surrealist meteorological iron-work close to the cliff side (GPS N 42°39 667: ED44°33 505 Altitude 3040 metres). We lunched quickly and hurried down – but the walk should have continued another kilometre or so, up the cliff. Remember you need a GOOD three hours to descend from here (we took four due to a late afternoon cloud-clearing that generated far too-many-than-is-healthy, photo-stops).

Back. The way you came.

2 Day option. Continue beyond the head of this walk, up to the edge of the Gergeti glacier at about 3400 metres then (with the assistance of a guide) cross the ice and con-

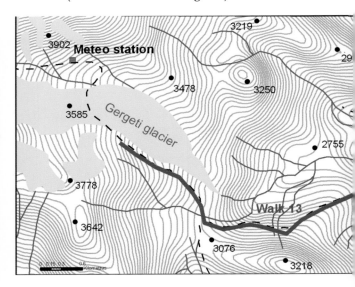

tinue to the Meteo Station at 3652 metres and spend the night. You must bring food and a warm sleeping bag.

Gergeti glacier and Mt Kazbek

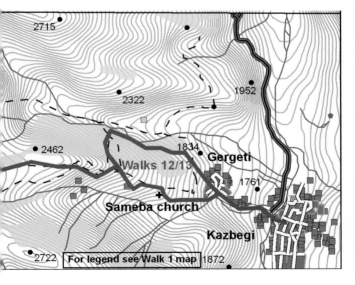

JUTTA

INTRODUCTION

The village of Jutta stands at 2150 metres. A small cluster of houses at the end of a long, climbing dirt road at the junction of two valleys. One continues on towards Chechnya, seven 7ms to the east (now heavily guarded and behind high peaks), the other to the spectacular Chaukhi mountain. Said to have only two hours of sun in mid-winter, Jutta is inhabited by Khevsurs (more peaceful and pagan than the drink-loving Mokhebe). When I asked my guide how many families lived there he said 'one - Arabuli.' By this he meant that virtually all inhabitants are from various branches of the same family.

Chaukhi mountain is seen on the way in, poking above the neck of the valley, slate grey and ribbed, in one long jagged summit. To me more like a massive Victorian organ at the head of a treeless and utterly barren valley. The village is incredibly cold in winter, because the tree line here is much lower than in Kazbegi, and on the northern, sunless side of the mountain ridge. Inhabitation has been helped by a gas supply, piped in from the main trans-Caucasian pipe in the valleys below.

Walks 14/15 ═══════

CHAUKHI MOUNTAIN

Start/finish - Jutta village, 50 minutes from Kazbegi.
Type - One way return
Dates - June to end of October (snow may restrict Walk 15)
Time - 3 hours and 7 hours
Upward climb - 400 metres and 1000 metres
Max elevation - 2575 metres (Walk 14) 3050 metres (Walk 15)
Grade - Easy (Walk 14). Moderate but strenuous (Walk 15)
Mobile signal - None

Summary

Two memorable walks in a remote valley – one a fine aperitif to a memorable main course. In both the goal is visible virtually all the way – the magnificent Chaukhi mountain, the Caucasus's answer to the Dolomites. The peaks appear as a row of stiff, rocky fingers scratching at the sky at the end of a bleak and treeless valley (Walk 14). Few easy walks in the Caucasus are so consistently spectacular. In (Walk 15) you continue on, traversing a steep incline alongside these organesque columns of rock, ending right next the eastern-most – close up to this rock-climber's paradise (one of the peaks is called 'Cameron' after its first climber, a British woman). The vertical, slate-grey cliffs seem higher than they in fact are - 3842 metres. But this lack of altitude permits the feel of intimacy. Walk 15 ends at around 3050 metres, resisting the 3338 metre Roshka Pass – to give adequate time for photos and return. When I took this walk – late September – we were bathed in sun, snow, hail, rain all within an hour – as the Chaukhi peaks swirled in and out of cloud. A full-on Nature-show. By then the Roshka Pass was already under snow.

Route

Climb through Jutta village following the track straight up from the right hand side of the bridge at the bottom of the village – short-cut under the bent gas pipe to avoid centre of village and dogs. A stick is handy to threaten the sometimes loose dog that rushes up. Above the village is an occasional football pitch with wonky goal posts and no nets (I doubted any game proceeds beyond 1-0, as the scoring ball would plummet 150 metres into the valley below). The walk evens out into a spacious bare valley – an easy stroll on the left hand side of a small river (although this can be partly covered in avalanches up to mid July). Toward its head cross the river (now a stream), near a small waterfall, then on up to the Climber's Camp (GPS N 42° 33 263: ED44°46 208 Altitude 2575 metres). You can drink the water straight from the stream as it emerges, fully filtered, from the moraine base, about 200 metres away. No chance for pollution by cattle. Thus ends Walk 14.

Now for the main-course…

Walk 15. This begins by continuing along the path toward three giant purple rocks where it sheers off to the left and up. The track comes and goes all the way up to the end of the valley, climbing quite steadily. Since the destination is less important than the view on the steadily closing-in Chauchi massif, the path isn't vital – but makes life a lot easier. The golden rule is – *never cross the river* - even though it seems to want it at first, Keep the main river always on your left and follow the path whenever it re-appears. Your goal is a mount at the far right hand (eastern) corner of the valley, beginning at the end of a green slope at (GPS N 42° 33.438: ED44°48 132 Altitude 2980 metres). The walk officially ends on top of the hill rising up from the stream above this green slope (GPS N 42° 33.340: ED44°48 207 Altitude 3050 metres). But if you have time (and no snow) you can climb higher.

Back - the way you came.

3/5 Day option. Continue up over the Roshka Pass and down to Roshka village and/or onto Shatili, the spectacular 9th century stone town in the centre of Khevsureti, on the Argun river, near the Chechen border. These require overnights, tents, guides and horses – but are wonderful.

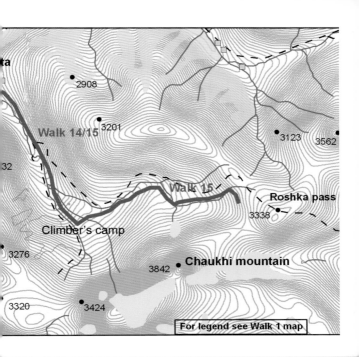

Chaukhi mountain

TRUSO

HISTORY

The Truso gorge offers an interesting example of successful blending of Caucasian nationalities. The territory is Georgian, yet Ossetians (with their Persianesque language) have lived in the valley for centuries. While Georgia and Ossetia are still in dispute over territorial sovereignty, these people just get on with life – displaying, to my mind, a superior psychology to the near-sighted politicking responsible for so many territorial/language and identity disputes across the Caucasus. Tolstoy also found these emotions and customs fascinating and wrote about them in his 'Hadji Murad' (about a Chechen leader who befriended the Russians). Today, for the most part, the Ossetians speak Russian - the most recent lingua-franca of the Caucasus (although English is now starting a take-over).

Walk 16 ═══════

TRUSO GORGE and VALLEY MINERAL LAKE

Start/finish - Okrokana village at entrance to Truso gorge.
Type - One way return
Dates - May (when show melts) to November
Time - 4-6 hours depending on how far up the valley you go.
Upward climb - 150 metres
Max elevation - 2175 metres
Grade - Easy, unless choosing to wade the river
Mobile signal - None yet.

Entrance to Truso gorge, near K

Carbonated lake

Summary

Walk begins in the Truso gorge (best in autumn when the trees are brilliant yellow and red), then follows the Terek river into the geo-gas curiosity of the Truso valley. Just inside is a bizarre naturally carbonated lake – Co2 boiling up to the surface as if in a permanently shaken Perrier bottle. The pool is rimmed by brilliant red iron deposits, which run down to the main river like open veins. Perfectly safe to visit, but don't camp next to it on a still night – you may suffocate. Nearby numerous mineral springs have laid down carpets of white, yellow and orange sinter deposits blended with iron oxide, to decorate the valley floor. Further up, at a village called Abano ('baths' - due to a former hot spring), comes heavy whiffs from nearby sulphur bogs. Find them by following your nose. You can see the bubbles sitting on the surface of what look like dirty brown pools – but the water is gin clear (drinking not recommended). The valley is also inhabited in the summer by Ossetians – formerly all the year round, as evidenced by a number of half-ruined 11th-14th century towers and homesteads – the best are at Ketrisi and Abano (the valley's first and second villages).

Route

Turn off the Georgian Military Highway at Almasiani village, at the base of the Jvari ('Cross') pass road (near Kobi). The Truso Gorge begins 2.5 kms later at Okrokana village. Start walking here – along the jeep track. Spectacular cliffs soon rear up on the left hand side. Don't miss the shrine to St George, with wishing tree, right on the road, near the gorge end (its about 2kms long). Once out and in the Truso valley, keep following

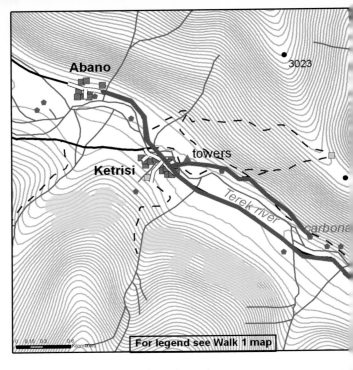

the jeep road, over the white sinter terraces, then just after two stone graves on the left look right across the river for the boiling carbonated mini-lake – at the base of the mountainside, (directly opposite GPS N 42° 36 227: ED44°25 223 Altitude 2150 metres). In late summer the river can be waded. If not, you must walk all the way up to the Ketrisi village bridge, then back down. Since this involves several extra kilometres, the walk officially ends at the mini-lake (since you must back-track the whole distance home). However, if wadeable, then the walk can continue on the lake-side of the river, all the way to the Ketrisi village towers, then along the jeep track to the Abano village towers (and cemetery) before turning back.

2/3 day options. Hike south, up from Abano village onto the 3000 metre Volcanic Plateau with its wonderful coloured lakes. Then, if you want, on and down into the Aragvi river valley, to Gudauri. Requires tents, food, guide etc. Stunning.

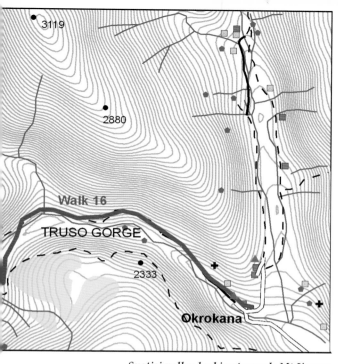

Suatisi valley looking towards Mt Jimara

Walk 17 ━━━━━━━━

TRUSO – SUATISI VALLEY

Start/finish - Suatisi village (or opposite it in June/July)
Type - One way return
Dates - June to end of Oct (best Aug – mid Oct)
Time - 5 hours
Upward climb - 400 metres
Max elevation - 2500
Grade - Easyish
Mobile signal - None.

Summary

Walk along a flat river valley toward an orgy of spectacularly high mountains, glaciers, needle peaks, snowy plateaus. Unfortunately during our walk clouds covered most of the orgy, but the few tantalising glimpses of spiked peaks peering through waving chiffon clouds made it worthwhile. On a good day this route up behind Mt Kazbek gives excellent views of Mt Jimara (4780 metres); the accompanying glaciers and parts of the Kazbek plateau at 4500 metres) Few walkers venture down this lonely valley - preferring to stay in Truso or head up left to the spectacular Volcanic Plateau (requiring at least one overnight in a tent). I like it as a good, empty place to clear the head of city fug and prepare for the more dramatic walks of Kazbegi or Jutta. One advantage is you drive through the Truso gorge then up through the valley past Abano, stopping at key sites along the way (see Truso walk) before beginning, in effect covering both walks.
Note: this walk is river/road dependent. The 2100 metre Truso valley can open late and is only sparsely inhabited in the summer. In 2005 the road in didn't open until August due to a landslide (very unusual). I've never done this walk in late spring, but would like to try, as the Suatisi river must be wild…

Route

You need to drive in and up the Truso valley (see directions Walk 16). The start of this walk depends entirely on *when* you attempt it. In June or July the road to Suatisi village (which requires fording the river) will almost certainly be impassable due to melt-water. In this case you can only walk up the *right hand side* of the Suatisi valley. Start at the ruined Zakagori village and tower at the mouth of the Suatisi valley. Climb up behind the ruins then down into the valley on the far side (avoiding the river directly underneath the watch-tower). Then simply follow the river all the way up the valley to the top. At one point – directly opposite Suatisi village (the valley's only habitation) – you must climb the hill about 30 metres to avoid a river cliff – then gradually descend. Later in the year you can start the walk 2 kms further up at Suatisi village – which shortens it to give more time at the spectacular valley head. Once there I would advise climbing up the left-hand escarpment a few hundred metres to improve the view. Keep your eyes peeled for 'jikhvi' the western Caucasian tur high up on the mountain, the male with its distinctly curved horns (see photo pg 17). The eastern Caucasian turn has straighter horns like the Ibex. **Back** – the way you came.

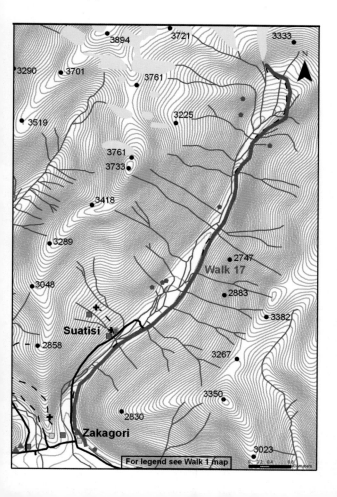

MYTHOLOGY

The Georgian 'jikhvi' or Caucasian tur has been a staple hunter's goal for thousands of years. In pre-Christian times one of the principal mountain Gods was called Dali, also known as the Goddess of the Hunt. Legend declares that she provided good and bad luck to certain hunters, depending on whether they slept with her. One in particular, Mepsey, refused, but later shot a gold-horned 'jikhvi' which bought on his terrible luck. It was believed the Goddess sometimes took on the form of this mountain goat. Unusual looking goats in the herds were often spared in the hunt for this reason. Photo pg 17

Devdoraki glacier surface, at the top of Walk 19

DEVDORAKI GORGE and GLACIER

Start/finish - Gverleti village (8 kms north from Kazbegi)
Type - One way return
Dates - Mid May to November. Best June/July
Time - 4/5 hours and 9 hours
Upward climb - 550 and 1200 metres
Max elevation - 2300 and 2650 metres
Grade - Easy (Walk 18). Difficult (Walk 19)
Mobile signal - Only at start

HISTORY

These two walks step directly up out of the famous Daryal Gorge – the historical route through the Greater Caucasus. Celebrated by painters, poets and composers for its drama – this gorge has witnessed the passage of numerous armies – including the Romans, Mongols and Russians (and nearly the Germans in 1941, who were stopped near Vladikavkas, 35 kms to the north). For a long time no more than a bridle-way it was enlarged into the Georgian Military Highway by the Russians during their expansion southward at the end of the 18th and start of 19th centuries (dreaming of retaking Constantinople for Christendom). At times extremely narrow and deep, it has enabled handfuls of men to stop whole armies in their tracks. When the Russian poets Lermontov and Pushkin came in the early 19th century (see 'Hero of Our Time' and 'A Journey to Erzerum') – travellers could only pass through in large, heavily armed convoys. Valleys like the Devdoraki branch off to the side, formerly providing hide-outs for the bandits. This region is frequently depicted in 19th century romantic paintings (like Lermontov's) and pre-revolutionary tinted photographs - some found in the museum in Tbilisi's Caravanserai (by Sioni Cathedral).

Summary

A fine walk along the southern flank of a massive canyon leading to the Devdoraki glacier – which tumbles down from the white Kazbek plateau, hanging in the sky at 4500 metres. One of the (more difficult) climber's routes up Kazbek, it is also less commonly walked by tourists. The short walk is relatively easy yet provides the feeling of great drama without too much exertion – and the sensation of walking through a rock garden. The longer walk expands the drama significantly – ending up on the clean white ice of the glacier surface, having crossed five avalanches. The short walk ends at the edge of the first avalanche (at about 2300 metres) – but you need a jeep (it cuts out the first 350 metre climb from Gverleti village). The long walk merely requires a lift down the famous Daryal Gorge (celebrated by Mikhail Lermontov in his poem 'The Demon' – see **History** above) along the Military Highway to the hamlet of Gverleti (easier and cheaper to arrange) – and a lift back to Kazbegi (we hitch-hiked without problems). The short walk requires a lift up the beginning of the Devdoraki valley. If the walk is made in September the avalanches may have melted – but the sides are still steep and hard to negotiate (especially the second). Note – bring waterproofs because at one point you walk under a small waterfall.

NOTE. If you drive down to the Russian border it may still be closed to foreigners (whether you have a Russian visa or not). Only locals can cross. Near it is a Russian fortress.

Route

The route for both walks is the same – the long one simply extends front and rear. Drive 8 kms north from Kazbegi down the Military Highway to Gverleti (3kms from the Russian/Georgian border). The start of the long walk is the jeep track turning left at Gverleti, immediately before the first bridge after Kazbegi over the river Terek (GPS N 42°42.627: ED44°37.590 Altitude 1430 metres). Just follow it all the way to the end (1 hour). At the top you arrive at the nexus of two huge valleys; the left is Devdoraki. On the short walk you drive this section. The path is now clearly visible climbing the valley wall to the left - but begins not by the World Wildlife sign but slightly fur-

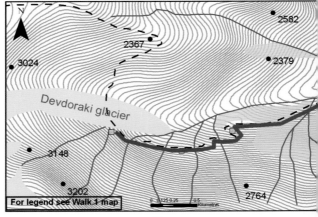

ther along just below the metal snow bucket (GPS N 42°42.520: ED44°35.683 Altitude 1775 metres), where you double back. The path is good, built to service a former copper mines further up. Follow it for two hours plus, up to just above the tree line and the first avalanche cliff. Here the shorter Walk 18 ends.

Walk 19 continues up the side of the avalanche, climbing above the ruined miner's house (beside a pond to the left) until you spot the path continuing on the other side of the snow (GPS N 42°43.026: ED44°34.333 Altitude 2300 metres). Then cross the avalanche – I suggest kicking into the snow and using a stick for support. Four more avalanches remain (unless walking in late summer when the avalanches may have melted) until you arrive at the delicious white dome of the main Devdoraki glacier - the walk's goal. Always climb up to the level of the path continuing on the far side – then cross. At avalanche 4, head for the ruined hut. By the fifth you're well up beside the glacier, the clear ice isn't far. Here you must find your own directions – constant movement of the glacier will change all co-ordinates. Make sure you walk onto the glacier where it is relatively flat – the ice is slippery (we descended onto the glacier around GPS N 42°43.100: ED44°33.451 Altitude 2500 metres). Don't go too far, or up the glacier – where the crevasses begin. But the dome is fine, Stay off the glacier if covered in fresh snow – it could conceal a crevasse.

Back – the way you came. Don't dally on avalanches or under high cliffs as boulders occasionally crash down.

Note for a Medium Walk. One option is to drive to the start of the Walk 18 (cutting out the first 350 metre climb along the jeep track) then do Walk 19 (now 7-8 hours).

Waterfall: At Gverleti a small river rushes down to join the Terek from its west side. Follow this up into the mountains for half an hour and stand before a large and worthy waterfall.

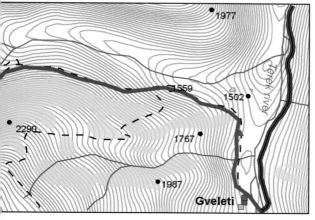

DAVID GAREJI

INTRODUCTION/HISTORY

To visit the monastery at David Gareji is to follow the footsteps of a man (its namesake) who left the 6th century civilisation to start life as a monk in this remarkable semi-desert setting. Choosing a cave under a huge sandstone cliff that collected water in pools (and later cisterns) for the long summer months, his new home looked out on a painterly landscape of orange, red and yellow sandstone – filled with birdlife. Since his initial journey, thousands of monks have made exactly the same choice, so that by the 12th century, the David Gareji complex formed the largest monastic environment in the Caucasus (in its heyday inhabited caves could be found in a 20 km radius). Today virtually all are abandoned, however the original desert atmosphere survives, especially up in the Udabno ('desert') caves on the ridge top. The walls are painted with 10th - 12th century frescoes above the now re-inhabited Lavra monastery, but scrawled with graffiti from the Soviet period - when this area was used as a military training ground.

Walk 20

To the UDABNO CAVES

Start/end - Lavra Monastery
Type - Loop
Date - All year
Time - 2-3 hours (depending on time spent in the caves)
Upward climb - 200 metres
Max elevation - 875 metres
Grade - Easy but occasionally steep
Mobile signal - Partial

Summary

One of Georgia's more special tourist attractions, this classic short walk takes in an abundance of sandstone colours, 12th century frescoes, birdlife, and silent semi-desert landscape. The initial steep climb puts off some tourists; and the rumours of snakes many more.

to: Looking down on
ra monastery

Yes snakes do live in and around the caves, but many are not poisonous. One however, Lebetina Vipera, is and quite common, (see Fauna section for ID photos). If nervous avoid April, May, June – unfortunately the best season as the desert turns green and everything celebrates; flowers, insects, birds, mammals, reptiles. I personally just walk carefully and in numerous trips have only seen one snake. Add this to the extraordinary frescoed Udabno caves and the picturesque Lavra monastery below – and this walk stands out as truly memorable. Once up at Udabno I highly recommend just sitting down and listening for several minutes. The place is teeming with wild-life, and is one of the best birder's destinations in the country (see story below). Apart from the virtually resident Egyptian Vulture (April to October), with its splendid white plumage, you begin to notice the lizards, turtles, and the many smaller birds.

Route

Walk from the car-park up to the Church shop before the Lavra Monastery entrance. Immediately afterwards a rough sandy path climbs steeply up to the Lavra tower above. This is the start. Walk up to the tower then just where the path starts to head down toward the monastery, turn directly up the hillside following another path (continue on down and you do the walk in reverse). Climb steeply up for some 15 minutes until you encounter the rusted mono-rail beside a path. This is your guide rail (literally) up to the ridge top then down the other side to the Udabno cave monastery. Once found you cannot go wrong. The rail's support posts even continue the length of the monastery, leading almost to the rebuilt chapel at the head of the ridge. This marks the end of the caves and the start of the descent down to Lavra. A path runs diagonally away from the chapel down the hillside, facing the large bare sandstone hill, with its carved-out water channels, eventually to the rear entrance of the Lavra monastery. Do not try to enter the monastery. This is the private reserve of the already tourist-harassed monks. Instead cut up round the back of the small wooden outhouse to some steps which then climb up the hill until a track bears off to the right. This will take you back to the tower overlooking the monastery – where you initially departed from the path and cut up the hill. Head down to the car-park.

**FACTS ABOUT SNAKES.** Snakes hibernate in holes throughout the winter – November through to March. They're primarily nocturnal and most active, mid April/May.June, when they mate. Young are born in August. Be cautious when reaching over rocks. If concerned bang ground as you walk – they feel the vibrations – and _**walk slowly**_. Snakes are generally rare in Georgia bar a few hotspots. In 18 years visiting the Caucasus I've heard of only one person being bitten – a Georgian art historian sleeping in the caves at David Gareji. He survived 'but with some discomfort.'

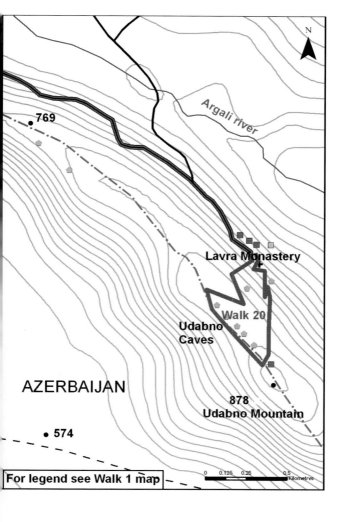

MONASTERY OF BIRDS

The Georgian lettering on the small, scrawled sign read 'Gareji...' We'd taken the right road.... Finally the Niva lifted its squat nose up onto the plateau from the dusty Rustavi basin. Then everything changed. Silence flattened the air around the jeep now gliding through a sea of yellow grass. We stopped for a moment, shut off the engine and all sound extinguished with it... until gradually that other engine - nature - raised its volume... Skylarks. This high, watery voice of the sky came in from every direction – light and incandescent. The birds seemed as happy as us to be away from the city, remote from the smokestacks of the Guldani power-station still just visible in the haze below. Small and brown they perched on posts by the roadside singing at full blast – welcoming in our solitary expedition. Nothing could be further from the honking, race-track of Tbilisi. No more speeding cars, advertisements, the forced auto-mental-shut-off of the city. The road stretched away into an empty, treeless, highland. Just grass, more grass and sky.

Instinctively our senses attuned to the new environment. A place not of sunglasses but binoculars. And quickly came a clue that this place was indeed special. The nearest Skylark wore a small feathery tuft on its head. Not the common Skylark of the UK, but the more exotic Crested Skylark – singing its beak off.

Fifteen minutes later another clue. A huge bird, lopping its wings lazily just above the ground and soaring off down the valley. A quick register of its white under-wing-fringed with black identified it as the dignified Egyptian Vulture. One of the smaller, more elegant vultures known for its snowy white plumage – and according to the book 'Raptors of Georgia' an estimated 120 pairs still exist here. We watched it glide over the green escarpments like a black and white patrol car, meandering where it wished, scouring the ground for infringements of natural law.

But no sooner had it departed than a flash of brilliant turquoise skimmed through the sky…. Way too big for the only flying turquoise I knew – a Kingfisher. Then a glimpse of something fantastically multi-coloured moving inside a bush. Now not only turquoise, but yellow, red and blue. In a kind of rapture we stopped the car, lifted binoculars. Surely not a bird?

But it was… and something quite unique for those of us bred in the UK countryside. An exquisite rainbow-fantasy of a creature, with long, pointed-beak, head flicking side to side. Why did nature press so many bright colours into a single mammal? What earthly point, save perhaps to delight us? Later a bird book confirmed this as the European Bee-eater.

And the David Gareji enchantment kept coming. As we passed the first 12th century monastery (its caves painted with frescos in as many-coloured as the ground outside), the roadside flowers condensed into a living killim of colour. Yellows and purples dashed together with the red of poppies – and then the turquoise bird again, posing, only metres away on a post. Later I confirmed it as my first Roller. Larger than the Bee-eater, with a shorter beak for stabbing at seeds, this time I lifted my camera and released the shutter.

'Got him,' I head myself say – sounding eerily like a hunter bagging his first grouse. I glanced at my friend, only to find him staring straight back.
'Peter…' he said, 'I think you've just become a bird-watcher.'

BORJOMI-KHARAGAULI REGION

INTRODUCTION

The deeply wooded, Borjomi-Kharagauli National Park is the largest and most developed National Park in Georgia (76,000 hectares or 1% of Georgia's total land-mass). But 'developed' only in the sense that a part is sectioned-off as a full-on nature reserve with marked trails, mountain shelters, an official guide structure, a visitor centre and information pamphlets. Set in the heart of the Lesser Caucasus the experience is more deep forest, than open mountain side. Trails are designed for walkers, birdwatchers, botanists – not sports holidays. Much credit must go to the World Wildlife Fund and German government for funding this pilot project for the rest of Georgia's National Parks. The Teutonic organisation is appreciated both by the wildlife (bear and lynx numbers are starting to stabilise after over-hunting) and would-be walkers – who can stroll along marked paths with a greater confidence (assuming the trails are maintained once funding ends).

Geographically it is different to the other mountainous areas as the altitude is lower – the highest peak in the Park is only 2642 metres (highest walk 1750 metres) – so can be walked virtually all year.

The Park has many marked trails c/o the **National Park administration** (found at 23 Meskheta Street, on the far side of Borjomi, about a 15 minute walk from the centre towards Likani. More details at **www.nationalpark.ge**), but most involve carrying sleeping bags, food, etc with over-nights in one of several remote tourist shelters. If this is your bag (sorry)… check their website,

NOTE: Walks in this region originate from *different accommodation points* – on either side of the park – unless you choose to do the excellent 2/3/5/6 day walks, travelling from one side to the other staying in the wooden shelters.

LOCATIONS

These walks have two main points of departure - Borjomi and Marelisi (you must choose in which to overnight). Both areas have accommodation and are easy to reach.

Borjomi is a two and a half hour drive from Tbilisi. Marshrutkas are plentiful from Didube station, Tbilisi. Once there taxis and hotels can be found in the town centre.

Marelisi, the centre of the Kharagauli section, is a two hour forty minute train ride from Tbilisi (main station) on the constantly improving Tbilisi-Batumi line (terrible roads make driving very slow and unadvisable). A marshrutka (mini-bus) usually meets the train to drive the 6 kms up to Marelisi village, but taxis are usually available too. To take the pleasant river-walk to the Marelisi Guest House, turn right out of the station, cross the river bridge, take the first left, following the river *all the way*, past the school until you meet the unmistakable new Guest House with its large, green Borjomi-Kharagauli Park sign. Gia, the caretaker, lives in the house above.

BORJOMI

HISTORY

Borjomi's history as a spa and nature reserve begins in the 19th century, after the Russian arrival in Georgia. Marked out as a potential health resort by the Grand Duke Michael Romanov, brother of Tsar Alexander ll, development began in 1872. The villa in Likani was built in 1895, then a hydro-electric station and water-bottling plant.

Borjomi water soon became famous across Russia (and remains so today), and the health spa hosted the likes of Tchaikovsky and Chekhov. Its National Park also has the same beginnings, firstly as a game reserve for the Russian aristocrats. A part of the forest was fenced off and wardens established. Many of the same delineations are used today.

Photo: In the virgin forest of the Borjomi Kharagauli National Park

Walk 21 ━━━━━━

LIKANI VILLAGE to the KVABISKHEVI GORGE

Start - National Park entrance above Likani village
End - National Park exit above Kvabiskhevi village
Type - Single direction, one way
Date - March – December
Time - 6 hours
Upward climb - 850 metres
Max elevation - 1750 metres
Grade - Medium
Mobile signal - Start, end and on top only

Summary

A fine beech/pine forest trek with ridge-walking (mostly amid trees) at the top, then down into a beautiful volcanic-cliff canyon. A well marked walk, although some of the higher signs looked precarious, so taking along a local guide is preferred. This walk has the advantage of being designed c/o the Borjomi-Kharagauri National Park Visitor Centre (23 Mesketa Street). The Centre is en route so drop in for booklets, maps and information (although skip their Informational Walk which at present is designed for children). Better is their website - **www.nationalpark.ge.** However nothing beats a local guide for about 30 lari a day – c/o the Visitor Centre, in advance).

You may be asked to pay small amounts for the booklets – but worth every penny as these are currently the best available on Georgia's flora and fauna.

Route

Take a taxi to the clearly marked Park Entrance above Likani Village at the west end of Borjomi (around 7 lari). Follow track to the trail '1' start sign; next to a wooden, designer picnic shelter. Follow the clear path up to the top - about 3 hours (any splits are short cuts). Top is easily identified by an oblong clearing, a bench and indicators; one pointing to the right - for the Lomistmta Tourist Shelter, and one to the left indicating trail '6.'

Turn left and follow '6' which is also marked by a black/yellow/black stripe on trees, however not as clear as '1.' The path sometimes disappears, but the rule is, 'if in doubt follow the ridge.' Having said this, the path soon comes to a clear divide – where you *must not* follow the ridge. A yellow/black marker on a tree below guides you onto the descending path. But this soon picks up another ridge with sudden stunning views. Keep 'following the ridge' down and up. When the path disappears you soon find it again. Eventually you come to a sign indicating a path heading away *down* to the right (soon

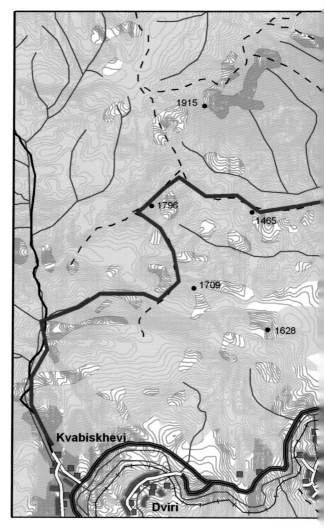

very steep). Take it – and it turns into another ridge. At this point better be warned that if needing a taxi for pick-up at the trail end – the mobile signal disappears once off the top here. It will take about an hour and a half from here to the National Park exit in the Kvabiskhevi gorge. Call now. From here the new rule is 'keep heading down' – if the path splits or you meet another one. This will lead you into a delicious open pasture, thence into the gorge, announced by a spring beside a picnic table. Turn left and stroll past the dramatic cliffs. The entrance gate arrives in about 20 minutes,

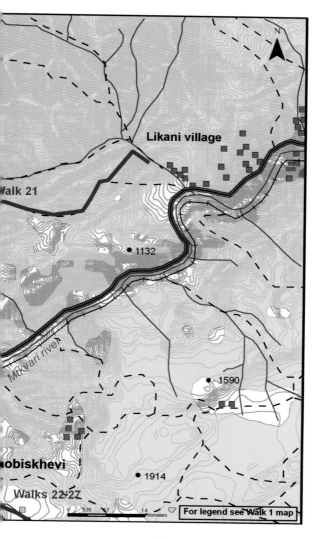

Walk 22

The DABATSZVALI LAKES

Start/end - Chobiskhevi village (12 kms south of Borjomi)
Type - Partial loop
Date - April to December (or all year but with snow on the top)
Time - 5-6 hours
Upward climb - 900 metres
Max elevation - 1800 metres
Grade - Medium.
Mobile reception - Not bad, except over the Sadgeri ridge

Summary

A steady 900 metre climb up from the narrow Mktvari valley to wide open summer pastures and pictur-esque Dabatszvali lakes (some locals may think you're saying Tsabaskuri lake – some 50 kms away to the south, so practise the ending). Two contrasting landscapes with the beautiful small lakes as a fine reward. Descend down the dramatic Mother-in-law's Tongue path – due to its sharpness – to make a small loop. Total walk distance about 15 kms – 9 kms up along the jeep track, 6 down care of the steep short-cut path.

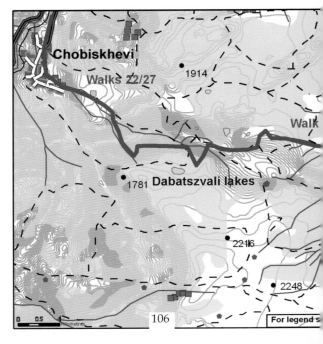

Route

To save an hour have the taxi/car drop you in Chobiskhevi village then simply follow the main street up. The way is

Dabatszvali lake

blindingly obvious (sounds like famous last words, but isn't…) along the access jeep road to the upper summer pastures and lakes. If in doubt look up and see the metal chairs hanging in the sky nearby from the defunct lift. On top the cutest lake hides away to the far right hand side (south), surrounded by trees. Take a dip if you're tough.

Down. Return to the cable-car head station then head to the right (north) about 50 metres and you'll see the Mother-in-law's Tongue path, It more or less follows the chair-lift straight down to the jeep track. If you want to make the loop in reverse – up the Mother-in-law – look for a path leading off to the right by a small grass triangle, about three quarters of the way up (GPS N 41°44.540: ED43°32.610 Altitude 1440 metres) where the road makes a left hand turn (tricky to spot).

NOTE: If wet the Mother in Law is not recommended.

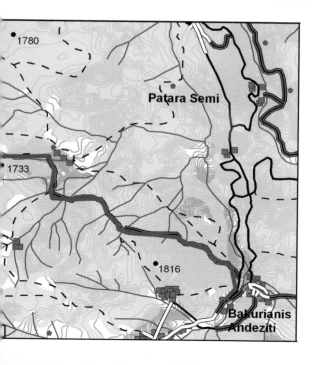

MARELISI

INTRODUCTION

Stepping out of the train at Marelisi station, after the hustle of Tbilisi is the first moment of pleasure. Warm wooded mountains rise up on all sides and the place just oozes relaxation. You've just arrived in the more sub-tropical west Georgia and your home for the night must be the Imeretian village of Marelisi (unless Georgian Railways add an evening train at Marelisi, or you decide to drive the terrible road in and out). But this is another real pleasure, because the village atmosphere is so authentic and virtually self-sufficient. They even stone-grind their own corn in small, communal watermills called 'tiskvili.' I stayed at the new Marelisi Guest House which is easily found (see Borjomi-Kharagauli LOCATIONS). It is clean and has 4 double rooms. The caretaker, Gia, lives in the house immediately above. To extend the shorter walk by 1+ hours walk up from the railway station, perhaps lunch at the Guest House (they will need some warning), then do the main (shorter) walk. For the long walk you need to start at dawn.

Walk 23

BJOLISKHEVI RIVER
(one walk, two distances)

Start/end - The Marelisi Guest House
Type - One way, return
Date - All year
Time - 4 or 10 hours
Upward climb - 200 or 800 metres (totalled)
Max elevation - 600 or 1050 metres
Grade - Easy or difficult with river wading
Mobile signal - None

Summary

For ionisation… This walk follows a wild, thrashing, mountain river the entire distance (bar one deviation on the longer option). The shorter walk is relatively flat

Photo: the Mar Guest H

and uneventful but you feel mysteriously invigorated. The path is a wide jeep track, all the way; impossible to get lost, so great for conversations (you may have to shout over the river) or thinking. You walk through varied woodland – with a slightly more tropical feel than the Borjomi side of the Park (it starts 400 metres lower). You pass waterfalls, springs, a wide variety of plants/trees, cross on cute double logged bridges – until after about two hours you arrive at the high, fine waterfall on the right, and a 'greasy pole' across the torrent, followed by some river wading. Hopefully this may change – for effectively this ends the trail for regular walkers. The pole is tricky, and the river wading demanding (over knee deep in a strong current). However I mastered both – by crossing the pole bare-footed (for grip); and wading the river Caucasian style (trouserless) and using a stick for balance. After this the road climbs away from the river then down again to meet it. Two and a half hours later you arrive at your goal, the unmanned 'Tourist Shelter' (sleeps 12), deep in the heart of the forest. Lunch. Definitely a *long* walk.

Route

Follow *the road by the river* up – then follow it down again.

Take these words literally and you cannot fail. Where options are offered, simply repeat these words to yourself.

PERFUMED PATH

Striding alone down the jeep track beside the Bjoliskhevi river - heading deeper into the Lesser Caucasus. I've been at it for several hours. The side of the path is dotted with flowers of every shape and colour. Occasionally the air is lit by the perfume of a large lily (Lilium szovitsianum), its head like a yellow face peering up from the roadside. Now I know where to look and can smell them from about 30 metres. Around them are numerous other wild flowers and I wonder if any are among the 300 supposedly endemic to Georgia. I've just crossed the river bare-foot on a greasy wooden pole, then had to wade across it again, water half way up my thighs (breaking my own advice about swift streams above knee-level as unwadeable). Suddenly a high waterfall appears on the right; casts a fine white spray over a lip of rock, then tumbles into space. With it comes an abrupt new feeling of great intimacy with this place. Myself among the steep, wooded mountainsides, river-water piling around rocks, a nameless peak peering down through clouds. It feels as though I've just passed through an invisible gate, entered the design studio of someone or thing far more intelligent. That all around whole species are being manufactured; developed, the patterns of flowers, rocks, butterflies, improved, touched-up – and I've no idea at all how its done,. In fact I could be just one more of those designs moving across an invisible story-board, being observed, studied perhaps even to be discarded…

I look ahead and realise I've no clear idea where this trail leads. Yesterday someone told me it just follows the river into the mountains and I could do the same. Eventually there might be a Tourist Shelter but I'd never make it in one day. So there was a challenge… Yet for the last three hours I've seen not one other human being. So where am I headed?

But right now I feel it hardly matters. It's so easy to trust this path. Follow the river up for half a day, then down for the other half. Walks don't come any simpler. I lift my camera, aim it up at the unknown peak. Suddenly I'm acutely aware of myself standing there amid the oak and hornbeam, a mere speck by the river in new hiking boots, hat aiming a telephoto lens. Is it not equally likely all this takes a photo of me?

Walks 24/25 ━━━━━━

To VAKHANI CASTLE

Start - Marelisi railway station
End - Marelisi station (Walk 24). Marelisi Guest House (Walk 25)
Type - One way return (Walk 24). Partial loop (Walk 25)
Date - All year
Time - 5/6 hours both walks
Upward climb - 500 or 650 metres (totalled)
Max elevation - 875 metres
Grade - Easy (Walk 24). Easy but complex directions (Walk 25)
Mobile signal - Virtually permanent

Summary

Two village walks through steadily elevating country-side, up to a small 12th century castle keep. There you look down on Georgia's pastoral heartland, see the numerous, individual homesteads, mostly self-sufficient, dotted across the landscape. Pass vineyards, the small, water-powered corn-mills, multi-cropped fields the majority being worked. The National Park looms dramatically to the south. Both walks have an identical first two thirds – up to the Vakhani castle then back down to Vakhani village centre – mostly along jeep tracks (save the final push up to the castle). Then the choice is either head back the way you came to the railway station (then take taxi or mini-bus to your accommodation), or deviate to the left for the 'deep village' experience. Travel along pony tracks, beside streams, down into dells, winding through a labyrinth of pathways, past numerous highly individual homesteads until finally regaining the Bjoliskhevi river, thence to the Marelisi Guest House. Directions are given here – but complex, so a local guide is recommended if choosing Walk 25 (or leave plenty of extra time). To find a guide contact the National Park Visitor Centre (**www.nationalpark.ge).**

Route

Step off the train at Marelisi station and start walking to the left, along the gravel road beside the railway. After forty minutes you arrive in Vakhaiskikhe hamlet, where after crossing a river you see a green metal 'village kiosk,' beside a right hand turn upward. Take it and some 200 metres on, when it forks, choose the lower jeep road and continue for another hour into Vakhani village centre (recognisable by its concrete-bus stop, basket-ball patch and shop). The school is just round the corner to the left. Follow the road past it, until it divides. This is important. (GPS: N 41°56.888; ED43°18.971)

Both forks head up to the castle, but the lower, left hand fork is best, and leads towards a picturesque corn-mill cabin ('tsiskwili'), built over a stream. This is where the villagers grind their dried corn ('simindi') into flower, later to become 'chadi' or corn bread. Note the naked corn-stack poles sticking out of lone trees along the way as the castle-hill looms closer overhead. The road passes a small pond; rises more steeply; encounters some turnings; but *keep climbing* until arriving at a T junction beside a corn storage house. Turn right. 150 metres on, at the jeep track's highest point, a path leads straight up and to the left, (GPS N 41°56.815: ED43°19.812). Ahead is an old, balconied, wooden homestead, walk past then bear right directly behind it. This is the path to the castle. You can either take the direct route, straight up, or stay on the path and meander up. Both take you to the top. A spring is found about 30 metres below

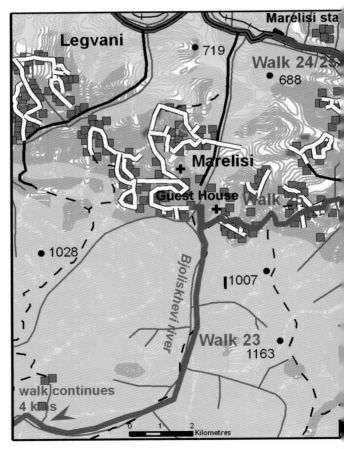

the top, now piped, but water leaks out.

Down. Return the way you came to Vakhani village centre, then either continue all the way back to the station (Walk 24) then take a taxi to your accommodation, or head straight for

Tsiskvili

the Marelisi Guest House (Walk 25) and into the deep village experience. You cut away from Walk 24 by crossing the river in the village centre, beside the bus-stop, now on the left hand side. Then directions become complicated. 150 metres on, take left hand fork and follow the jeep track up the hill to Serbaisi village. Continue straight through on *up* to the crest of the next hill (GPS N 41°56.865; ED43°17.849). There do not head left on up into the mountain but straight

down the other side toward the houses. At the picket fence turn right down a small bridle path. 100 metres on, at the T junction among the picturesque homesteads, turn left along larger path. 100 metres on, at next T, turn right. 100 metres on, at next T, turn left (near spring pipe). At bottom meet small river, which you follow *down all the way* to the main Bjoliskhevi river at the bottom. There turn right and the Marelisi Guest House is 1 km on downstream, beside the river. Tricky but possible. Becoming lost on this walk isn't dangerous because so many houses surround you. You can always just ask for the way to Marelisi.

BAKURIANI

INTRODUCTION/HISTORY

One hundred and fifty years ago Bakuriani barely existed. Then the Russians began developing Borjomi down in the valley and needed a 'mountain retreat.' So in 1902 they constructed the narrow gauge railway all the way up to this then hamlet, even employing Gustave Eiffel to construct a bridge. Today a hamlet no longer, the Soviets developed Bakuriani into a ski-resort, with no less than three ski-jumps (it was even mooted as a Winter Olympics venue). After Georgia's civil war (1992-3) it fell into disrepair and is only now finding its feet. Set at 1650 metres in the Lesser Caucasus the atmosphere is less severe, greener than the high Caucasus walks (like Kazbegi/Svaneti). There are *many* fine walks directly out of Bakuriani village – here is only one. The second 'lakes' walk here is big, but beautiful, especially in October, with the fabulous autumn colours. For information on Bakuriani consult the excellent CENN website – **www.cenn.org**.

LOCATION

Eagle Owl

A forty-five minute drive up from Borjomi - taxis and mar-shrutkas (mini-buses) from the town centre. Or a 1.5 hour plus ride in 'kukushka' – the narrow gage train. Leaves twice daily from top and bottom. Plenty of hotels and home-stays available throughout the year. **The Bakuriani Tourist Information Centre** (run by the Tbilisi NGO, CENN) is located at 2 David Aghmashenebeli Street, right in the town centre: **bakuriani@cenn.org**.

Walk 26

KOKHTA MOUNTAIN

Start/end - Bakuriani centre
Type - Loop
Date - April/May to November
Time - 4 hours
Upward climb - 500 metres
Max elevation - 2160 metres
Grade - Easy, with steep climb up
Mobile reception - Permanent

Summary

This is the most obvious walk in Bakuriani. Kokhta mountain looks down on the resort town from every angle, clearly identifiable by its array of mobile masts and chair-lift head-station on its bald green summit. Kokhta means 'cute' in Georgian, but was obviously cuter – pre the mobile mast. The claim is that on a clear day all of the Caucasus from Kazbek to Elbruz are visible. However I've never improved on a few hazy bumps in the distance – but still an excellent, wide open walk, especially if taken slowly on a sunny day. The lower stretches down, involve a delightful, flower-filled forest. Great in autumn of course – for the spectacular Caucasian colours.

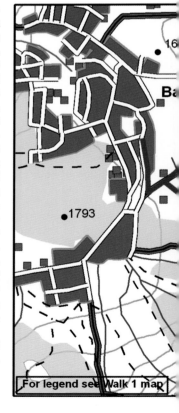

For legend see Walk 1 map

Route

Pretty easy. Take any road out of the town centre eastwards. They all converge on a single road that leads out of the valley. About 500 metres along turn right up to the Lotus Hotel and Kokha chair lift base station. Walk up under the hanging chairs then bear slightly left away from the chairs up through the open steep slope to the mountain top (carpeted in flowers, spring/summer).

Down: Simply continue on along the head-station access road – downwards. Just one choice – about ¾ down to the Bakuriani crater (it's an ancient volcano) the access road opens into a clearing and splits, (N 41°44.540: ED43°32.610). Take the road that heads up and to the left. This leads to the old, decaying ski-jumps, then finally down to the ring road. It is possible to do this walk in reverse. Just head for the first ski-jump head poking above the trees - across the open fields. Turn off the upper ring road beside a green painted hotel (GPS N 41°44.784: ED43°31.986).

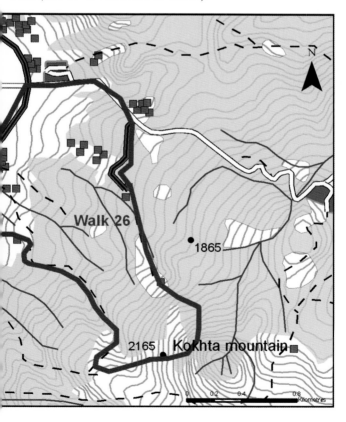

Walk 27 ▬▬▬▬▬

ANDESITI to DABATSZVALI LAKES (map pg 106)

Start - Andesiti village (4 kms west of Bakuriani)
End - Chobiskhevi village (12 kms south of Borjomi)
Time - 8 hours – 9 if wet
Type - One way
Date - April/May to November
Upward climb - 500 metres (downward 900 metres)
Max elevation - 2000 metres
Grade - Medium but long
Mobile reception - Not bad

Summary

A long but superb walk (especially during autumn colours) taking in a wide variety of lower-alpine landscape and pastures – up to the picturesque Dabatszvali lakes due west of Bakuriani (not to be confused with the larger, bleaker Tsabaskuri lake to the south). No hard climbs but ends with a steep and dramatic descent down to Chobiskhevi village thence the Mtkvari river. Total walk distance about 20 kms. The route begins by following a former logging road through dense pine forest to a wooded valley. Then slowly the way climbs up to a delightful open plateau of green pastures and small lakes. If you want climb a hill at the top and catch glimpses of the Baku-Tbilisi-Ceyhan pipeline as it summits over the lesser Caucasus to the south. Finally plunge down over the rim of the Sadgeri ridge to the warmer climate (fireflies in summer) below. Start *early*.

Route

Take a car/taxi from Bakuriani (usual overnight destination) west to nearby Andesiti village. Continue through village and immediately after crossing river at T junction take the higher right hand road, and have yourselves dropped (road is soon undriveable). Follow this former logging road deep into the forest with the mountain on left hand side for two plus hours (do not deviate up into the forest – as we did once with a local who quickly became lost. Avoid guides called Levan!) Eventually you exit the forest and head towards a small village. About 100 metres before the first house cross a stream and immediately take the path turning left into the woods, climbing gently up (GPS N 41°45.720; ED43°24.717 Altitude 1625 metres) . Follow this and the stream for about 40 minutes into a clearing, then spot a sort of path continuing on the far left hand side. If you can't find it, don't worry, just head due west into the wood. Staying on this bearing you will eventually hit a jeep track (a compass or GPS is nigh-on essential here, unless you have a good sense of direction). If you start heading down, you're going wrong. Eventually the jeep track opens out onto lightly wooded grasslands and meets a T junction. Bear left and soon it swings round to eventually hit the ridge top (GPS N 41°45.588; ED43°21.960 Altitude 1920 metres). The lakes and grass plateau are directly ahead and down. The three lakes lie ahead (there is a fourth pondish lake due north) with the best and largest lake on the far left (southern) side, not immediately visible, but beyond the southernmost sum-mer-pasture cabin. The descent down over the ridge is either by the jeep track or preferably, the more dramatic Mother-in-law's Tongue path (due to its sharpness). This begins just to the right (north) of the defunct chair-lift head station. From here the route is pretty Mother-in-law, but easy in direction - down all the way to Chobiskhevi village (1.5 hours). *Avoid the Mother-in-Law if wet.* The steep path meets the jeep track about half way down (GPS N 41°45.909: ED43°20.007 Altitude 1440 metres). The village is long and thin. Head on through it down to the bridge over the Mtkvari river and the Borjomi-Akhaltsikhe road (another half hour). Marshrutkas (mini-buses) run every half hour back to Borjomi during daylight hours. From Borjomi taxi or marshrutka back up to Bakuriani.

Kvelo tower looking down on Dartlo

TUSHETI

INTRODUCTION

Tusheti is the remote, top right hand corner of Georgia, next to Daghestan and Chechnya. Although only open four months of the year, a whole world exists up in these four valleys, its population still living in ways similar to several centuries ago. While a number of villages now stand abandoned, those still functioning cling determinedly to mountainsides between 1800 – 2200 metres, and are populated devoutly in the summer months. A few are still occupied through the long, isolated winter, but only by two or three hardy families. Each village is dominated by a revered pagan shrine ('khati') – which in fiercely Christian Georgia hints at an unusually independent culture. But it *is* fragile. The Soviets bought electricity to the region in the 1970s until it disappeared in 1985, never to return. Today there is talk of installing mini-river generators, as still very few houses have their own petrol-powered ones – producing enough power just for light and charging mobile phones. But for the last (very recent) detail and the occasional satellite dish perched on the winter houses (there is no radio in Tusheti), the villages have hardly changed for centuries. Locals survive mostly on cattle herding and the locally grown potatoes, harvested during the brief summer season. In autumn they ship their famous cheeses (regarded as the best in Georgia), wool, organic potatoes, down to Tbilisi. In wintertime the houses are closed as owners retreat down to Alvani, in the warm, Kakhetian valley.

The most significant 21st century addition to the region has been the arrival of Georgian border guards, monitoring the mountainous Chechen border. They are supported by helicopters which occasionally chop their way across the deep valleys and do not take tourists (except in emergencies).

HISTORY

To enter Tusheti you must cross the 2917 metre Abano pass – the highest road in Georgia. Considering this car access was only completed in 1978, and remains open from just late June to mid October due to snow, it's a wonder any kind of human culture exists up in this remote, but stunning region. However, iron animal figurines from the 5th to 4th century BC have been found buried close to Tusheti's many black slate towers – themselves dating back to the 12th-13th centuries. These resilient, stone fortresses are key to the Tush's survival. Constructed on steep hillsides, to defend against raids from the Chechens and Daghestanis, they come in two forms; the watch-tower - to alert villagers of imminent attack, and the larger, squatter, communal towers – into which entire villages would flee during assaults. Interestingly, they also display two quite separate roof designs, one with a double pitch, the other bee-hive style – indicating the cultural diversity between these mountain communities. The first are found most obviously in the now restored old Omalo fortress, the second in the upper Birikiti valley – Dartlo, Parsma, Girevi - as well as across the mountains in Chechnya.

NOTE: I was told it costs only about $3000 to restore a Tusheti tower, using local craftsmen. One hopes restoration will continue – following the excellent example set in Omalo (privately funded by a Dutch businessman).

The 'khati' in Dano

SALOTSAVI - 'HOLY PLACES.'

The Georgian Orthodox Church has made only slender inroads into Tusheti. I know of just two churches, one long-ruined in Dartlo, and one now being renovated beside the more revered 'khati' in Shenakho. The 'khati' are pre-Christian shrines and are still venerated by villagers. Women are forbidden to enter these sanctuaries (including tourists) – a feature common to animist cultures. Also called 'salotsavi' (holy places) each one is dedicated to a local saint (formerly a God), usually unknown to outsiders, but some have been Christianised. Several 'khati' are dedicated to St George, although on closer investigation one discovers both a 'black' St George (associated with the local God Lashara) and a 'white' version, closer, one assumes, to the one we know. Clearly linked to ongoing animistic beliefs, the 'khati' are easily identified - small piles of stones, often bedecked with animal horns, candles and always topped by a white crystal. One of Tusheti's main festivals is Lasharoba – which takes place about 100 days after Easter in Shenakho and Chirho villages.

NOTE: In summer Tusheti has a number of village festivals associated with different saints. The last is Mariamoba (dedicated to Mary) held around the 28th August.

LOCATION

The only way in is by jeep over the Abano pass (about 7 hours from Telavi to Omalo). Currently no minibuses or public transport. If rich you can hire a helicopter at about $2000 – one way (the Russian MI8s seat up to 20). But this is complicated and best arranged through local tour companies – see page 10 (as are the jeeps). Some people try catching lifts on the huge Kamazi or Zil trucks that lumber up over the pass – but they're highly uncomfortable, unreliable and difficult to find. They also often break down.

Walking in Tusheti

Without doubt Tusheti is one of Georgia's finest walking environments. It is lower and greener than other high Caucasus areas. It also feels safer than Svaneti – the only other comparable Georgian region. Trekking alone I feel more relaxed than in western Europe (due also to the absence of fellow trekkers). The people are more easier-going than the Svans. I've never heard of a robbery in Tusheti. The mountains are more benign too, less snow and drama – the pastures flatter, the avalanches less intense. The population is also far smaller and still, for the most part, animist. In autumn the Tush emigrate down to the warmer, wine-rich Kahketi, but this produces a yearning for the spring and a return back 'up' to the homeland - by then carpeted in flowers. For botanists and birders Tusheti is a haven. Tourism is very undeveloped, but accommodation is easily found in friendly homestays. The more visitors arriving in a village, the more houses open their doors. Tusheti is now registered as one of Georgia's National Parks, and a plan for a visitor's centre and proper museum, some guest houses and marked trails is being formed. In the meantime Tusheti's mountains are ribbed with cattle-paths and huge flocks of sheep that hoover up the grass at virtually every altitude, tended by aggressive Caucasian dogs – which are best given wide berth (see Dogs, page 15). Mobile phone communication has recently arrived – also handy – but the signal (at the moment only the Magti system) comes and goes without much logic.

NOTE: Female walkers are requested not to approach the 'khati' – small stone piles topped with a white crystal, with a recess for candles. In villages the 'khati' sanctuaries are usually fenced off. Some have a stone wall and resemble churches (as in Parsma). If encountered during a walk women should come no closer than about 15 metres. This sometimes means an awkward detour on mountainsides – but must be observed if walkers are to remain welcome in Tusheti. Photographing the 'khati' is fine.

CHURCHKHELA

This is Georgia's superior answer to trail mix. A combination of nuts (either walnut or hazel) and grape paste, it is eminently transportable and tasty. When blood sugar dips this combination of glucose and protein slowly releases into the blood and helps you over the pass. Traditionally a Khahetian invention, it can be found in local markets across Georgia (not in any supermarkets yet) – although the Kakhetian churchkhela are reputedly the best.

SHENAKHO to DIKLO

Start/enld - Shenakho
Type - Loop
Date - June - October
Times - 4 hours and 5 hours
Upward climb - 350 metres
Max elevation - 2175 metres
Grade - Easy (Walk 28). Medium (Walk 29).
Mobile reception - About two thirds of both walks

Summary

Great introductory walk to beautiful Tusheti, leading to one of my favourite places in all Georgia, - the ruins of the Old Diklo fortress (**Walk 29**). You perch on a massive cliff-top overlooking Daghestan, with a 1000 metre drop below. Behind is the quaint Diklo village and valley, to your left the white pyramid of Mt Diklo jamming into the sky. To get there you walk through a pine forest, pass near to an ancient, but well preserved watch-tower, then either climb either straight up to Diklo (**Walk 28**), 'the last village in Georgia' (not strictly true as one Daghestani occupied village stands beyond). or climb a fairly steep hillside to the Old Diklo fortress perched on the most extraordinary rock promontory, with a view to match (**Walk 29**). Both treks end with a leisurely one hour stroll back down a wide grassy valley to Shenakho. Note of warning – we encountered some particularly aggressive dogs around a shepherd's hut on the level path walking back from the fortress to Diklo. No harm done, but nerves were shaken. They could be avoided by walking back down the hillside to the **Walk 28** trail (way you came) then climbing back up to new Diklo, but it adds another 150 metre climb. I personally would risk the dogs again (see Dogs, pg 15).

Route

Walk down the hill from Shenakho on the Diklo path, start climbing the other side, but about three quarters the way up, a lesser path leads away to the right, (GPS N42 22 601; ED45 40 013 at 1950 metres) heading towards a smaller ridge (gap between two sets of trees). Take it to the ridge. *Do not* follow another path then branching off to the right, heading into the trees or you'll end up in a Georgian border guard camp.

Descend from the ridge to the stream, which you follow past the ruins of an old corn mill or 'tiskvili' [to see them working do the Marelisi walks, see pg 108], then off to the left into the forest. Apparently corn was once grown in the lower valley ahead. In about 400 metres the path divides, take the lower route – then just keep walking for about 45 minutes along a more-or-less level forest path. Eventually you enter a small 75 metre wide clearing where the path disappears. But don't panic, the way is simply *up* through the clearing. Soon you see the ruins of some winter houses, then a path into a wider flatter pasture (GPS N42 23 244: ED45 41 747 at 2050 metres). At the far end (left side) pick up the forest path again, it runs along the side of a canyon, watch tower looking at you from across the gulf, the old Diklo fortress clearly visible perched on a cliff-top directly above (destroyed by the Daghestanis in the mid 19th century and never rebuilt). This path will lead all the way up to Diklo (Walk **28**).

Walk 29, the more dramatic option, follows this path to just beyond where the tower disappears and you see the path divide (GPS N42 23 683: ED45 41 933 at 2010 metres). Take the lower branch leading down to the stream and follow it some 150 metres until a valley climbs up to the right. You can see the old fortress so just climb the valley towards it (no path) bearing right after about 100 metres through the sparse trees. Your destination is the top, far right (GPS N42 23 782: ED45 42 141 at 2175 metres) – and the stunning fortress view. Train your binoculars on the high Daghestan ridge about 6 kms east above the deep Charma valley, and spot the Russian border guard training his on you. Apparently they're forbidden to sit, must stand and look for two hour shifts. Enjoy your khajapuri. To return, walk back along the ridge top until meeting a levelish path leading away to the left, towards Diklo. This takes you all the way to the village. Here is where you could meet the gnashing dogs (see Summary) – so be prepared. Walk through the centre of Diklo – women avoiding the khati (identified by the large white crystal stone on the top) - and notice how there are no pigs in Tusheti villages. Tushes don't eat pork while in Tusheti, but do so outside. Beyond the village a clear jeep track leads down the valley all the way back to Shenakho (about 1 hour).

VAZHA PSHAVELA

(1861 – 1915)

Behind the buried gloom of night
icy, pale to the eye
Chechnya is a bare rocky throne.
In a gorge below the river roars
its seething, inward wrath.
The mountains bend down,
wash hands, faces in the spray,
the souls of dead men
living on their flanks…
… in the distance appears a Chechen village
perched like an eagle's nest
and as beautiful to observe
as a woman's breast.

These are the opening lines from Vazha Pshavela's poem 'Host and Guest.' Regarded by many as Georgia's finest and most original modern poet, Pshavela lived in the high mountain area of Pshavi, next to Tusheti. Both cultures are very similar. I would describe him as the mountain walker's poet. His poems exhibit a haunting animist strain and concern themselves almost exclusively with the mountain villagers, their lives and relationships within the cavernous valleys. Osip Mandelstam, the celebrated Russian poet who visited Georgia, said of Pshavela's work in 'A Word or Two about Georgian Art.'

'His imagery, almost medieval in its epic majesty, contains an elemental force. It seethes with the concrete, the tangible, with everyday reality. Every utterance inadvertently becomes an image, and yet the word does not suffice – he must rip each word to pieces as it were, with his teeth, making the most of the passionate nature of Georgian poetry.'

For a good academic background on Georgia's rich literary tradition – see **'The Literature of Georgia'** by **Donald Rayfield.** This book is usually available at **Prospero's Bookshop** in Tbilisi – 34 Rustaveli Avenue.

The above is extracted from **'Georgia in the Mountains of Poetry'** *by* **Peter Nasmyth** *(me…), 3rd edition published by Routeledge; 2006.*

Walk 30 ══════════

OMALO to SHENAKHO
(or visa versa)

Start/end - Omalo or Shenakho
Type - One way
Date - June - October
Time - 1.5 hours
Upward climb - 350 metres (from Omalo)
Max elevation - 1950 (Shenakho)
Grade - Easy
Mobile reception - On top, but poor in canyon

Summary

A quick, often necessary walk between the two key villages of Tusheti. Divided by a 250 metre deep canyon, the river at the bottom must be forded by vehicles. Sometimes in the early summer the melt-water is too high even for the large Kamazi trucks, so this path and its footbridge is vital. The current bridge was built in 1965. If you're staying in Shenakho, it's pleasant to do this walk immediately on arrival in Omalo (stretch your legs after 6 hours of 4x4 lurching up over the Abano pass from Kakheti). Ask the driver to drop you at the trail head then drive your bags onto Shenakho. Don't worry, it's virtually impossible to lose your way.

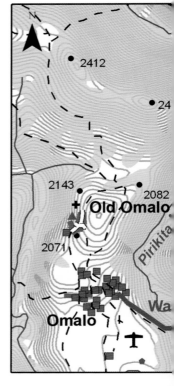

Route

Omalo start: Walk down from the village centre in a south-east direction past the current Border Guard barracks, towards two unfinished concrete buildings not far from the canyon side. The nearest is the never-completed cable-car head station begun by the Soviets. The path begins just to its left (GPS N42 22 030: ED45 38 413 at 1850 metres) and seems to divide after some 300 metres. Take the higher route then follow it all the way down to the bridge and up the other side. It crosses the road a few times but the ongoing track is easy to spot on the other side. Remember, if you find yourself walking down the road, you've missed it and won't be able to wade the river at the bottom! Once at the top on the other side, follow the road left across the pastures straight into picturesque Shenakho.

Shenakho start: Walk out of the village on the Omalo road to just before it enters the forest. You can see a path leading away to the right (GPS N42 22 092: ED45 39 162 at 1920 metres). Follow it down (it meets the road once briefly) then up the other side into Omalo.

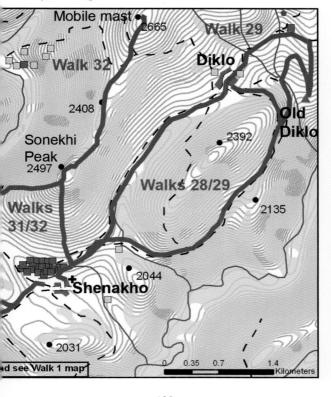

SHENAKHO to the SONEKHI RIDGE and MOBILE MAST

Start/end - Shenakho
Type - Part loop
Date - June to October
Times - 4 hours and 6.5 hours
Upward climb - 550 metres and 800 metres
Max elevation - 2700 metres
Grade - Medium (Walk 31). | Medium-difficult (Walk 32).
Mobile reception - Most of the way

Summary

A great walk for birders and those who like standing close to heaven – 'sonekhi' means 'lightening strike.' A forest route leading to a fantastic 2500 metre peak from which you see nearly all of Tusheti. The climb is along a mountain ridge all the way which, although forested, offers sudden, stunning views in both directions. The walk provides a rich, intimate feel with nature as you duck among trees and mossy rocks, while climbing steadily. Lichens hang from pines like beards, and at the bottom a Black Woodpecker followed us, pecking out messages with his red skull-cap banging on tree-trunks. I wanted to name this walk 'the Nasmyth,' due to my affection for it, but my companions reminded me this might be somewhat presumptuous in an area as ancient as Tusheti. Still, it has become a routine for every Tusheti visit.

Walk 32 merely continues on along the same rising ridge, which climbs out of the trees up along toward the Shavkvishtana ('black sand') ridge that peaks at 3200 metres. This is nigh-on impossible to reach in one day due to the initial slow forest route – so I've stopped the walk at the new mobile mast about three quarters the way up. But the super-fast could easily keep going.

Shenakho

Route

Leave Shenakho on the Omalo road but after about 300 metres turn off on the jeep track leading to the right *and up* (GPS N42 22 207: ED45 39 372 Altitude 1950 metres). This eventually climbs into the forest then disintegrates. But don't despair, the rule from here and all the way to the top is simple – ***follow the ridge***. Keep heading left in the forest and you'll come to it, then just stay near or on. Two hours later you emerge from the forest 500 metres higher and hit the summit (GPS N42 23 168: ED45 39 762 Altitude 2500 metres), beside a memorial plaque to a Tush who died in the Abkhaz war. You can see why he must have loved this place. In the evening Bearded, Cinerous and Griffon vultures, Golden eagles, and/or various hawks, glide past on the thermals rising up from Mt Sonekhi's almost vertical western flank. Old Omalo fortress glows in the light directly below. The Pirikiti and Gometsari valleys open out to the west, Daghestan is clearly visible eastward, and the Chechen border-ridge to the north-west.

Walk 32 (more difficult) begins at this point. You can see your goal clearly - the new mobile mast about 200 metres higher and a kilometre and a half to the north. The *'follow the ridge'* rule can still apply – but is far harder. A sort-of path begins about 50 metres below (to the east) after the initial descent from the Sonekhi summit, which is easier. Finally you emerge above the tree-line and meet the path to Diklo beside another memorial plaque - to a Tush who was shot at this spot in 1967. Don't take it, but keep going

Papakhi (hat) wearer

up and you will soon encounter a ridge-top shepherd's hut. Be careful – dogs won't be far. When they started barking we waited for the shepherd to emerge then waved and he then called them off. Only then did we head on. Drinking water in the shepherd's hut we discovered they looked after over 1000 sheep, which wolves regularly claim (hence the many vultures). Walk on up the steep climb to the mobile mast – admire the view, then return to the Sonekhi summit.

Down – both walks. *Do not* follow the ridge. Instead choose a direction about 45 degrees east (or left - towards Shenakho) from the ridge and head down. There is no real path. Pass through the sparse trees and eventually you will come to the wide open grazing flanks of the mountain. Shenakho village is clearly visible below. Head down the open mountainside – straight for it. Some people find this descent more arduous than the climb – to go slowly, rest, enjoy the fabulous view. The descent can be done in 45 minutes – but better to take an hour.

Walk 33 ▬▬▬▬▬▬

<u>DARTLO to CHESHO via DANO</u>

Start - Dartlo
End - Chesho
Type - One way
Date - June to October
Time - 4.5 hours
Upward climb - 400 metres
Max elevation - 2150 metres
Grade - Easy-medium
Mobile reception - Patchy

<u>Summary</u>

Walk begins with a visit to the classic Dartlo village by the Alazani river at the bottom of the Pirikiti valley. It winds up beside the 12th-14th century towers then makes a stiff 350 metre climb to the dramatic Kvavlo hamlet directly above - identified by its single watch-tower breaking the skyline. The route then parallels along the mountainside, past various homesteads to the remote village of Dano with its spectacularly pagan 'khati,' adorned with horns, set prominently on the village plateau. The path then runs along the mountain flank before slowly descending down to the valley floor from where it follows the increasingly isolated jeep road to Chesho village (and its accommodation).

<u>Route</u>

Walk up through Dartlo village (1800 metres) to the highest house, where a path leads upward to the left. It then switch-backs up into the grass meadows where you climb straight up until meeting the main path to Kvelo. Follow this all the way (further than it looks) to the tower (GPS N42 26 622: ED45 35 215 at 2150 metres). Behind the tower is Kvelo hamlet and a clear path leading away to the west, more or less level. Take this all the way to Dano village – negotiating the dogs at 'Governor' Gela's homestead on the adjacent hillside. Notice the 'khati' (dedicated to Yaksari) sitting on the hill above

fortress at Old Omalo

Kvavlo village. In Dano make sure you visit the splendid 'khati.' The village is also home to the famous Tushetian singer – Lela Tataraidze (I strongly recommend her CD of Tushetian songs). From Dano the path cuts round a gully, crosses a stream, then about 200 metres on, divides (GPS N42 27 036: ED45 33 894 at 2130 metres). Take the lower route. This then gradually descends down to the road by the Pirikiti Alazani river (GPS N42 27 914: ED45 33 158 at 1900 metres). Follow it west and within an hour arrive in Chesho. This last co-ordinate will help those trying to do this walk in reverse – the path is very hard to spot (and describe) leading up from the road.

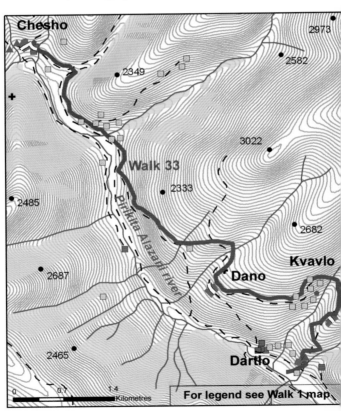

Walk 34 ━━━━━━━━

GIREVI, HERHO and the LAROVANI LAKE

Start/end – Girevi, at opposite ends
Type - More or less one way
Date - June – October (harder during the July melt)
Time - 4.5 hours
Upward climb - 400 metres
Max elevation - 2250 metres
Grade - Medium (except for the wading).
Mobile reception - Occasional

Summary

We took this walk after the start of September when the river levels are low – because wading is involved. If you are able and willing to go knee deep in a fairly swift (and very cold) mountain river, the rewards of this walk are great. I personally find it invigorating and wade bare foot (stimulates the blood). You visit the splendid watch-tower at Girevi – probably the best in Tusheti – then cross two rivers below and climb up, past the death houses of the abandoned Herho village, then down and along the mountainside to the brand new, turquoise-coloured Larovani Lake, created a few years ago by a massive landslide, partially blocking a small valley entrance. At the far end of the lake we encountered what could only be described as a field of spring flowers (in September) and some elegant snow formations and bridges in a still unmelted avalanche on the far side.

IMPORTANT NOTE: In June/July and sometimes early August the rivers here are too deep to wade, sometimes even for jeeps to cross. However access to Girevi village is still possible on foot, along a narrow path leading under the cliff on the right hand side at the first of the two river crossings, before the village. Depending on the depth of the melt water, it may or may not be possible to cross to Herho village and Larovani Lake beyond Girevi. Remember that a jeep can cross deeper water than a human, and a good horse deeper than a jeep. Horses can be rented in Girevi at about $20 a day – and can be used as ferries. The other option is the Parsma-Larovani Lake walk below – crossing the river only once at the new bridge at Parsma, but you miss Girevi.

Route

The walk starts at the superb watch-tower on the far side of Girevi. Walk down to the river, not entering the village, find a suitably low-water place to wade (each year will be different). Look for places you can see stones the whole way across, and where the river current is slowest – usually in the wider places. Cross slowly, making sure each foot is secure before lifting the other. It's safer if you keep your shoes on and use a stick (this third leg has saved me at least once) – but I prefer bare foot. You can already see the dramatic Herhro village and tower perched on the spur between the two river valleys directly ahead. Walk straight towards it and cross the smaller river right at its base (GPS N42 29 971: ED45 28 084 Altitude 2025 metres). Climb directly up the ridge of the spur to see the death houses (just below the larger ruins of the main village) – some even with human skulls still on the shelves. In former centuries villagers would come here to die. Keep going to the watch-tower at the top. There is an easier path that climbs up the right hand side of the hill, but it misses the death houses. At the top you can see the turquoise Larovani lake away to the west. To the north the valley continues up to Chontio (the start of a great **week-long trek** to Shatili in Khevsureti). Climb

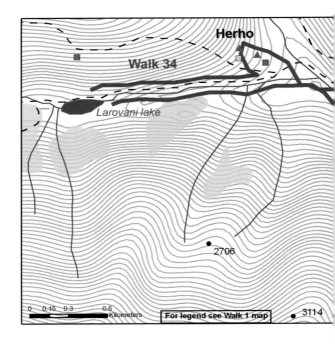

back down to the Larovani Alazani river but *don't cross it*.
Keep walking upstream beside the river bed then shortly
before a cliff makes it impossible to continue, you see a
path leading up the hillside to the right (GPS N42 29 970:
ED45 27 961 Altitude 2025 metres). This then follows the
river up to the lake about 50 metres above the valley
(swimmers beware, its ice cold).
Back - the way you came.

Avalanche at Larovani lake

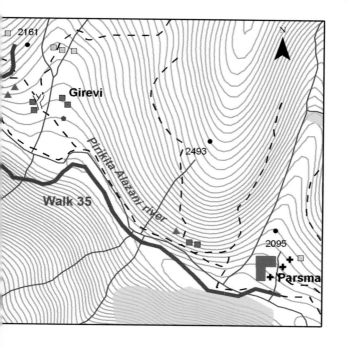

Walk 35 ═══════════

PARSMA to LAROVANI LAKE

Start/end - Parsma
Type - One way return
Date - June to October
Time - 4.5 hours
Upward climb - 300 metres
Max elevation - 2100 metres
Grade - Medium-difficult
Mobile reception - Occasional

Summary

A second-best, dry option to the above walk. You miss out on Girevi and Herho, but at least see them from across the river. The walk follows the Pirikiti Alazani river all the way from Parsma village to the Larovani Lake on its south bank, no wading required. Once at the Larovani Lake the way is difficult, walking on steep and loose avalanche shale. Opposite Girevi the walk climbs steeply up above the river, then continues for about a kilometre before descending down to the main river valley.

Parsma sheep

Route

Park at the base of Parsma village and cross the river on its new mini-Golden Gate bridge. Once on the far side the way is obvious – follow the river all the way upstream to the point of the second jeep road ford - into Girevi village. Here a steep cliff rises up on the left beside the river forcing you to climb the mountainside on the grassy spur about 50 metres before the road descends into the water (GPS N42 29 802: ED45 28 369 at 2010 metres). Climb about 75 metres then pick up the path that heads along the mountainside above the river cliffs. Follow this for over a kilometre until opposite the far end of Girevi village, then descend gradually into the river valley. At one point it divides (GPS N42 29 621: ED45 28 707 at 2080 metres), about bang opposite the *start* of Girevi village. The path starts to climb steeply, but about five metres up look for a smaller path running off the right. This is a weaker path, but saves you having to climb up high on the main path (I've no idea where it goes since we maintained our altitude on the smaller path). Once down in the river valley, *keep left* following the Larovani Lake valley all the way up to the huge land-slide, then scramble along the shale up to the lake.

Back; - retrace your steps

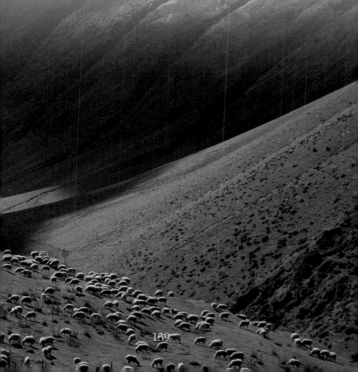

Lengeri

SVANETI

INTRODUCTION

The Svaneti district of Georgia contains the most dramatic walks in the Caucasus. To climb up from virtually any village is to enter a realm of permanently white and huge peaks, pastures of azalia, daisies, rhododendron, with 11th-13th century stone towers looking up from the valleys below. Set against this is a climber's world of high peaks (many over 4500 metres) and cliffs swirling amid the cloud. Not only is it a walker's gift, Svaneti is also a cultural centre, its many small churches housing some superb 12th century frescoes and icons – some now relocated to its several museums. Most Georgians regard Svaneti as not only the most beautiful part of Georgia, but also the most authentic. By this is meant the local traditions are more thoroughly preserved – this includes banditry. In 2003 the organised fleecing of a couple of tour groups led to the virtual cessation of tourism in Svaneti (except for individuals and climbers). Then in early 2004 the new Saakashvili government made a decisive statement. They flew in a helicopter swat team to 'take out' one of the key 'mafia' families – which they did in no uncertain terms. This sent out a clear signal that the centre would again stamp its authority on this remote region (as in the Soviet period). Thus in 2004 group tourism started again and by 2005 returned to normal. Svaneti is now back on the walker's map, but an undertone of wildness hangs over these villages. It is still not advised to wander round alone, take a local (Svan speaker) with you. But my experience still has the Svans as no less hospitable and friendly than any Georgians, but with the bonus of a quite stunning landscape. In no chapter of this book have I been more conscious of omitting magnificent walks as in Svaneti. It really merits a book in itself. However below are a few for starters.

HISTORY

Svaneti provides living evidence of Georgia's time-honoured technique of cultural survival. Located up long, rugged valleys, the many Svan villages have taken Georgia's finest treasures/icons during periods of invasion. Some valleys were never even found. The sturdy Svan towers rising from the ground like numerous mini-fortresses would have been a daunting sight to any invaders. The Svans are a proud and independent people.

They regard themselves as the 'first' Georgians – as their language 'Svan,' one of the four distinctive dialects of Georgian, is said to be closest to the original form of Georgian. Like most ancient languages, its origins are unknown. Some words carry similarities to Sumerian – but academics rarely posit more than vague links. Georgians from Tbilisi can't understand the Svans – but many will know some of the beautiful Svan songs and lullabies. Some are also used specifically for healing. The routes of Svanetian culture are extremely ancient and even appear to merge with Greek myth. In Homer's legend of Jason and his Argonauts, the Golden Fleece finds curious links with the Svanetian technique of panning for gold using sheep hides. Strabo describes the Svans as having a powerful army in the 1st century BC. Orthodox Christianity is strong in Svaneti but still pagan elements survive within local customs – like animal sacrifices and complex burial rituals. Many of Svaneti's churches have superb, 12th century frescos, one (in Lengeri) even has a 14th century pagan fresco (depicting Amirani slaying a Devi - mountain spirit) on the outside, The distinctive, crenulated Svanetian tower is unique in the Caucasus. Most of the traditional Svan families (names ending in '…iani') have their own towers, often several. These protect not only against avalanches but also fellow Svans, as the vendetta has yet to fully die. Mestia museum is definitely worth a visit, and when its open, the Ushguli tower museum.

Today Svans are among the poorest of Georgians and the region has been depopulating for some time. In the bad days during robberies the hooded bandits would often apologise to their victims saying that poverty had forced them into this. The irony of course is that of all Georgia's regions, Svaneti has the strongest potential for tourism – with its resultant economic gain. During my many recent trips I've had only good experiences in Svaneti and with the Svans – and sense that now the time is right for visitors to return in earnest - as they did, after all, in the Soviet period.

THE MOUNTAINS

Lording over all in the Mestia valley is Mt Ushba – a 4710 metre twin peak that hides itself tantalisingly from nearly all villages – save Becho and Mazeri. Described as the Matterhorn of the Caucasus this giant is one of the most attractive and deadly peaks in Europe. To watch and photograph, a superb mountain, but to climb, treacherous. Ushba's North peak was first conquered in 1888, but it took another forty two years and numerous attempts for the higher South peak to be claimed. Today

Ushba has over fifty routes but only two 4Bs (it's easiest). It is said to have over ten 6Bs (the toughest rating), including the famous 'sarke' ('mirror') on its North peak, a 1200 metre rock face some of it overhanging. Almost every year it kills. Svaneti also houses Georgia's highest mountain, Shkhara (5068 metres), accessed from Ushguli, and the beautiful pyramid mountain of Tetnuldi (4974 metres). Elbruz (5642 metres), Europe's highest mountain, is just across the border in Russia but views are blocked by high ridges. To see it, hike up to the Khalde pass from Ushguli (not in this book). For more history ask for directions to the Misha Khergiani private Alpinists Museum - that opens on request.

The book **'Classic Climbs in the Caucasus' by Friedrich Bender** – is also a good mountaineers guide, usually available in Prospero's café-bookshop, (34 Rustaveli, Tbilisi).

LOCATION

Svaneti is divided into Upper and Lower parts. This section refers only to Upper Svaneti, with its capital town, Mestia (population about 2500). An 8-10 hour drive from Tbilisi, the last five hours are bumpy but stunning, past the huge Inguri dam then following the thrashing Inguri river all the way up the valley to Mestia. Some people take the overnight train to Zugdidi, then marshrutka (mini bus) up to Mestia. You can 'marshrutka' all the way from Tbilisi but its gruelling. Most people hire a 4x4 and driver. A small plane flies intermittently from Tbilisi in summer, but is weather dependent. Accommodation in Mestia is plentiful but mostly in homestays – usually fine. A hotel is being built in the town centre, but currently stands unfinished. Homestays can be found through tour companies (see page 10), or personal contacts – many Tbilisi Georgians have Svan contacts.

Walking In Svaneti

As mentioned in the book's Introduction the high Caucasus have been inhabited and farmed for millennia. The result is a network of well developed often intricate pathways in the high mountains. The difference is – they are not marked, in the western sense – just known. Also due to the particularly high, steep valleys, some are avalanched or washed out in the spring – particularly higher up. Large hillside collapses can force major route-changes. Paths sometimes lead to sheer drops where sections of escarpment have caved in during the spring thaws. High pathways are not maintained (as say in the Pyrenees) they are simply adapted by the shepherds and cattle.

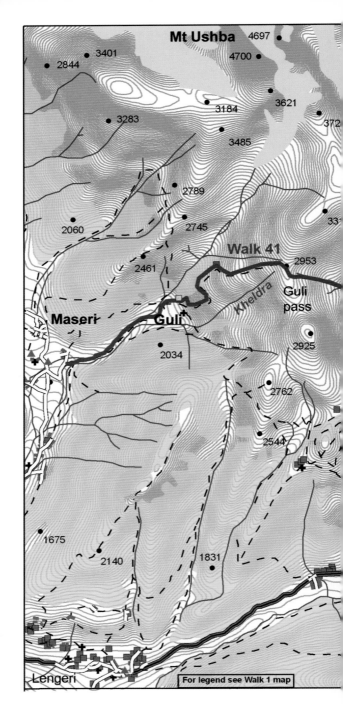

Mt Ushba 4697

4700

3621

3184

372

3485

3401

2844

3283

2789

2745

Walk 41

2953

2060

2461

Kheldra

Guli pass

Maseri

Guli

2034

2925

2762

2544

1675

2140

1831

Lengeri

For legend see Walk 1 map

144

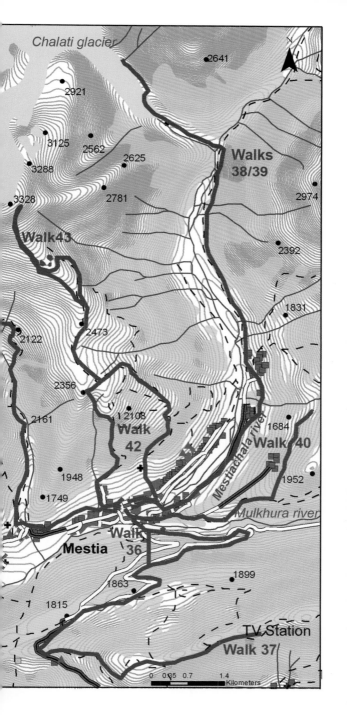

This means that for the higher walks, local guides are more or less essential. No GPS readings are given for Svaneti, partly because a local guide is recommended for security. Svans are traditionally suspicious of strangers. A guide is the important link to the community. I have heard of no robberies since the start of 2004 in Svaneti, and sometimes do small walks alone – but always prefer to take a local.

Mt Ushba (4710 metres).

In the early 20th century the local Prince Dadeshkeliani once gave this mountain to a beautiful German secretary. She had arrived with a climbing team – and the smitten Prince presented the mountain in the hope of receiving her hand. On her safe arrival back in Germany she is said to have returned the mountain to the Svans.

Walk 36 ═══════

The CHAIR LIFT

Start/end - Mestia
Type - Loop
Date - April to November
Time - 2 hours (max)
Upward climb - 200 metres
Max elevation - 1600 metres
Grade - Easy but a steepish descent
Mobile signal - Permanent

Summary

A short but satisfying walk for those with little time. It gives views of Ushba's summit (hidden in Mestia town), reaching up behind the Cross mountain; takes you past a splendid 75 metre sheer slate cliff above the roaring Mulkhura river, follows a jeep road most of the way up into the forest giving views over the town and valley, then drops you back down into Mestia under the guiding wires of a chair lift. Plenty of fine colours in the autumn.

Route

Head out of the main square on the Ushguli road. Cross both bridges, pass the large Museum and keep following the road. The houses soon end and the road climbs gently through the forest onto the mountainside above the wild Mulkhura river. After about fifteen minutes the dramatic slate cliff appears on the left, shortly after this the road divides. The lower heads towards Mulakhi and Ushguli, the upper toward Yeli and the TV station. Take the upper road. It climbs up through the forest, and soon you see the Ushba twin towers peeking down. Walk up about 25 minutes keeping your eyes peeled for chair lift cables crossing directly over the road. Once spotted, turn immediately right and follow them straight down the slope. You soon come to a cable tower - which dare-devils like to climb – then just follow the steep winding path down to a flatter area. Here you meet a path coming down from the right. You have a choice either to take this – which leads more pleasantly off to the left winding through the woods to the base station – or just to keep heading straight down under the cables to the cable car base. Once there you can continue straight on down into the village – but I advise bearing to the right along the jeep track to avoid the houses' guard dogs. The track soon arrives on the Ushguli road - so just turn left and walk back down into the town.

Walk 37 ━━━━━━━━━

To the TV STATION

Start/end - Mestia
Type - One way return (also potential loop with a good guide)
Date - May to October
Time - 6 hours
Upward climb - 900 metres
Max elevation - 2400 metres
Grade - Medium
Mobile signal - Virtually permanent

Summary

Among the best views of the Mestia region are gained from the ridge at the top of this walk. You stroll for a good 1.5 kms at the top of the world – and on a good day see all of Svaneti's highest peaks. For the more determined walker – a great first day introduction to the region. Of all the walks this is best rewarded by good weather. The route described here is all along the jeep track – although there are more direct, steeper and quicker routes which can take you in a loop. For these you need a good guide. I would advise the jeep track for one of the directions, as it passes through clearings to give great views.

Route

Follow the **Walk 36** route up to the point where you turn off the jeep track down under the cable-wires – then just keep going up on the jeep track. When it hits a small ridge follow it down into a shallow valley then up the other side. (don't turn left along the ridge), note the yellow azaleas whose perfume can fill the whole valley and Ushba's twin peaks that start appearing like a pair of rabbit's ears emerging from a hat. Climb up again until the road hits another flatter ridge with small fenced pastures on the right (and a couple of huts) where a steep road leads up to the left – take it. Don't continue straight or you'll descend to Yeli. Climb this steeper jeep track all the way to another flatter plateau, where the trees thin and eventually open into small pastures. There, more or less at the highest point, another left hand fork offers a jeep track up along what soon turns into the ridge top –

here the great views begin. Follow it all the way to the TV mast. Spot the dwarf Rhododendron Caucasicum (white/yellow flowers in June/July) along the summit. If desired you can continue along to the summit of Mt Zuruldi - add another hour.

Down – retrace your steps

Walks 38/39 ▬▬▬▬

To the CHALATI GLACIER

Start/Finish - Mestia
Type - Single direction, return
Date - May to October
Time - 7 or 10 hours (but depends on what lifts you take)
Upward climb - 300 or 600 metres
Max elevation - 2000 or 2300 metres
Grade - Easy (Walk 38). Tricky (Walk 39)
Mobile signal - Poor. Only at start (in Mestia valley)

Summary

A long, very pleasant one day walk – with an adventurous add-on, if required. This easy route takes you along the beautiful Mestia River valley with views of Ushba peeking down, up to the tongue of the Chalati Glacier. Then if you wish you can climb up the moraine side, towards the dramatic ice cliffs (better stay off the glacier surface). This second section should only be attempted by those with good balance and the patience to step on the boulders **slowly** and carefully – many are loose. However no special equipment is needed. If the second section is attempted it's advisable to drive all the way to the suspension bridge, missing the first flat section of the walk, to give sufficient time to reach the most interesting part – the ice cliffs – then walk back to Mestia (four hours). We took a lift half the way to the bridge, but ended up walking the last 2 kms back in the dark – all-be-it along tarmac road.

Route

Follow main (metalled) road out of Mestia toward and past the airport. At the end of the tarmac continue along the jeep track all the way to the head of the narrowing valley where the track ends (about 7kms). Just before the head you will catch glimpses of the Chalati glacier tumbling down from Chatin Tau Mountain to the left (where you're headed). To cross the river take the Soviet built suspension bridge just beyond the point where two rivers merge (don't worry I made it). On the other side follow the track left and up through the woods beside the Chalati glacier river all the way to the glacier tongue. The path is pretty obvious. Higher up the woods disappear and you can clearly see the glacier – so just follow the general direction. Note the significant glacier shrinkage markings painted on the boulders.

Walk 39. Facing the tongue of the glacier head up the steep boulder-cliff directly to the right. Stay off glacier surface. Once above the glacier, continue on along the right side, toward the ice cliffs about 2 kms up. Note the moraine boulders are often loose – so tread carefully and don't hurry. Coming down is more difficult – so leave more time.

Back - retrace your steps. It took us a full four hours back to Mestia from the ice cliffs – with no stops.

WARNING: Once at the glacier tongue, *do not* stand up close directly under the ice as large boulders periodically tumble down (especially on sunny afternoons) - as the ice mass melts - potentially fatal results.

Bridge to Chalati glacier

Walk 40 ══════

The ALPINE LODGE and PASTURES

Start/end - Mestia
Type - Partial loop
Date - May - November
Time - 3/4 hours
Upward climb - 300 metres
Max elevation - 1700 metres
Grade - Easy
Mobile signal - More or less permanent

Summary

An easy, aesthetic stroll up into the low alpine pastures at the eastern, dog-leg end of the Mestia valley. A good introductory walk affording fine views in two directions; one some 20kms westward down valley toward Latale; the other some 12kms northward toward the Daligora massif and Chalati glacier. All this of course under the watchful eyes of Mts Ushba and Tetnuldi, who gaze down much of the way. The walk is short and better extended by an hour or so, by following the jeep track on up toward the higher pastures – as far as desired, then back. This gives a good view onto the Chalati glacier northwards. Early deviations to the right, up to the rim of the dramatic Mulkhura chasm are strongly recommended.

Route

Head out of Mestia main square on the Ushguli road, but after the first bridge turn immediately left. Walk up the stony road, past the old Intourist Hotel (on right) choosing the right hand lane whenever the road divides. This becomes a pleasant amble beside small fenced/walled pastures. After some ten minutes bear in mind that just 50/100 metres to the right the great Mulkhura river chasm opens up with dramatic sheer slate cliff dropping away. Definitely worth a deviation and a peer-over at the great views up the river gully and of the 4974 metre pyramid of Tetnuldi. Be careful not to walk up to the edge without checking the rim first – some is just wads of turf with nothing below…

After this the track begins a brief switch-back and the sharp-eyed will notice a smaller path leading away straight up the hill. This leads to the ridge top and apparently gives a good view down into the Mulakhi valley –

but is a major deviation and not taken here. On this walk just follow the jeep track. After some 30 minutes you spot the ruined Alpine Lodge just down below – a powerful symbol of the Soviet period when Svaneti had been developed for tourists. The Alpine Lodge used to house 250 guests in its three tiers of rooms. The semi-circular restaurant with views over the valley give it a distinctive look. Before it is an abandoned swimming pool in a pleasant grass pasture – now used by resort-class cows. Here you have a choice – to walk down to the lodge then head back toward Mestia along its long entrance drive (making this a two and a half hour walk in total) – or continue on up - towards the higher pastures. The latter is advisable as it extends the walk and provides good views of the Chalati glacier under Daligora Mountain to the north. Walk along another half an hour or so (the choice is yours) then turn back. This way you can adjust the length of the walk – bearing in mind the trek back to Mestia's central square from the Lodge takes just under an hour.

Fresco in Laghumi church, near Mestia

Walk 41 ━━━━━━━━

MASERI to MESTIA – the GULI PASS

Start - Maseri village
End - Mestia
Type - Single direction, one way
Date - June - September
Time - 11/12 hours
Upward climb - 1400 metres (in one relentless go)
Max elevation - 2950 metres
Grade - Gruelling
Mobile signal - Poor until on top, or down in Mestia valley

Summary

This is an enormous, shattering walk – but fabulous. It brings you close up to the rock massif of Ushba providing vivid impressions of the most spectacular mountain in the Caucasus. As you make the long, arduous climb up toward the pass, the South peak looms ever closer and bigger overhead. You can see the climber's routes - following one some of the way - and then suddenly at the top of the pass (2950 metres), the Mestia valley opens up with all the high peaks stretching away. The descent is steep but not frightening. We followed the valley all the way down to the Inguri valley, then took a delightful track through the woods (above the road) to Mestia – impossible to describe this last bit here (I had a local guide, which is completely necessary on this walk). It's easiest to follow the main tarmaced road back to Mestia. This is a massive walk, some people take two days and camp up in the mountains. Guli means heart in Georgian – and you need a good one. Better do it when there is plenty of daylight (i.e not October) unless super fit and a speed walker. The directions below are only general because you should definitely take a local guide. I had one of the best, Zura, but still we had to back-track because of new land-slides. The walk climbs fairly high so altitude is a factor. We ran into fresh snow on July 1st just below the pass - so check on snow conditions first, particularly if in June.

Route

Start just before Maseri (a 50 minute drive from Mestia, up the Becho valley). Take the first right after the metal cross standing beside the road. Cross the river and walk up the valley between the two rivers, following the jeep track all the way to the ruins of Guli village, then up past its small church. Keep climbing and gradually swing left towards the looming cliffs of Ushba South. Keep following the alpinists' trail up into the huge empty valley headed by a small glacier, tipping down from Ushba South, which now looks increasingly enormous. Just before the final shepherd's hut turn right and head straight up the mountain, switch-backing up and up. After an arduous hour and a half, nearing the top, you should gradually bear right to hit the rim of a ridge (if you go too soon you'll be stuck under a cliff and have to back-track). You will see the flat Guli pass above, but first you have to traverse the head of a shaley valley to the grass, peat of the final push for the top, partially covered in snow when I went in July. By now I was definitely travelling on reserve, but fortunately my guide kept saying 'nearly there,' which tricked me to the top. The view is magnificent, and you can see the path heading left on up to the spectacular Coruldi plateau (one of the best views on Ushba available to walkers – but requires a night in a tent). The rest is downhill. More or less straight. The valley directly ahead leads down to the Inguri valley and is pretty obvious. Head down the centre of the valley, don't take the paths that traverse the sides – unless you want to walk on (and up again) to the Cross peak – then down to Mestia (left hand traverse). By then I'd had my fill of '*up.*' At the bottom you hit the Mestia road, where you turn left and walk the last few kilometres back home. The walk down is as big as the walk up (about 1500 metres) - so is hard on the knees. Do not attempt this walk unless you're hardy!

Mt Ushba route

Walk 42

The CROSS PEAK

Start/end - Mestia
Type - Loop of single-direction return
Date - May to October
Time - 4/5 hours
Upward climb - 900 metres
Max elevation - 2350 metres
Grade - Medium
Mobile signal - Permanent

Summary

A stiff but good introductory walk – offering superb views in all directions most of the way. The Cross stands directly above Mestia, you can see it from the central square, nearly 1 kilometre above. It stands proudly right in the crook of the valley dog-leg – so you can see virtually everything from the top. This is the start of another climbers' route toward Ushba, but the mountain is only clearly visible on arrival at the Cross. This is more than compensated by the magnificent panoramas of Banguriani, Daligora and Tetnuldi mountains for more or less the whole trip. Arrival at the Cross is a surprise as from the town it looks no more than a couple of metres high – in fact it's over four, giving a good indication of the altitude (and views) gained.

Route

As in all walks the start is important, but in this case fairly easily found. Head out of town on the wide, easternmost road from Mestia's main square – toward

Laghumi village. The road runs, dead straight about 300m, past the few shops then just before it bears slightly right and down toward the river bridge, another road branches up and to the left. Take it. This heads straight up into the old village, and is also the route toward the Tower and House Museum (well worth a visit). Walk straight up. There are choices, but 'directly up' is your guide. You should soon pass under an old stone arch connected to a tower, then on up out of the village. The last major right hand turn heads across to the Tower and House Museum – but don't take it. Keep going straight up the now increasingly steep open track, past a tiny chapel (to the left) up to the top of the stony water-escarpment where the path bears to the right. Here begins the best route to the Cross – and the climb loses some of its severity by taking a steady north-eastward route along the slope of the Cross hill, following the Mestia valley increasingly northward. The path is very clear (much used by cattle) and eventually joins the jeep road up to the Cross. Follow the road for a few minutes then, where it begins to bend away to the left, beside two gates to pastures (on opposite sides of the road) you have a choice. Either follow the jeep road all the way up to the Cross (simplest, but least rewarding) – or take the steep upward path leading away to the right. This climbs stiffly up but offers excellent views of Daligora and Banguriani mountains – all the way to the first huts of the summer village. Here the houses interconnect with paths, so follow one to the left and upwards. My favourite route from here is to continue on up, past more of the houses to the top of the ridge (now near), then, when you see the Cross, slightly below and to the left, walk down to it. Ushba is now clearly visible all the way. You can also follow a path down, through some firs, to pick up the jeep road again, then on up to the Cross. Both options start from almost the same altitude as the cross – so don't require a great deal of extra exertion.

Down – there are several options. One is take the jeep road all the way – this is longer but follows a different route, landing you further north in the Mestia River valley. Then simply follow it back through Laghumi village to Mestia. You can also just descend the way you came - along the path (which I prefer since you see the same splendid views again but from the other direction)... *or,* you can descend by another completely new, *very steep* path straight down into Mestia. This is quickest and ends up west of the town centre. It can be found by walking up the ridge a few minutes from the Cross while looking keenly left. A little way up you should spot a path leading down, then turning left again into the woods. This route is also fairly clear, but is enclosed by trees much of the way (giving sudden spectacular views). The direction is pretty easy since you can see Mestia town most of the way – to keep bearings. At the bottom you hit another small valley made by a stream – which doubles as a path, Follow this straight down to the main road, then turn left into Mestia town.

Walk 43 ═══════════

The CORULDI RIDGE

Start/end - The Cross Peak above Mestia
Type - Single direction return with loop mid way.
Date - July - September
Time - 7 hours (or 9 if walking back down to Mestia)
Upward climb - 900 metres
Max elevation - 3300 metres
Grade - Difficult and strenuous
Mobile signal - Permanent

Summary

Possibly the most spectacular walk here, but also most difficult and at times hazardous. Never a climb (no equipment needed) but often a scramble along steep escarpments. Altitude is also a factor – (noticeable from around 2500 metres) so you need to be fit. However, once up on that ridge... all is forgotten. The view onto the ice fields is simply staggering. You look down on two huge glaciers - the Ushba Ice Fall and Chalati glacier. The tower of Chatin Tau (4368m) rises up directly ahead like a Mt Doom – and lording above all is Ushba, now awesomely close. The place is so high – so absolutely not designed for humans – it catches your breath. Up there you are threatened by rock and ice on three sides; on the forth the vast empty space of Mestia valley opens up all the way to Tetnuldi. You also begin to acquire that mountaineers' acute sense of the weather. I was caught in a blizzard up on the ridge (see 'Story') which fortunately passed. But we didn't hang around too long as another approached. The quickest route up is clearly visible all the way, as the entire walk is above the tree line. However near the top the walk turns steep and difficult on loose shards of slate. Boulders flake away and can tumble down a 100 metres - so *never* walk directly beneath (or above) your companions. Before starting check on the snow conditions. Too much will stop you in your tracks – although a little is helpful for footing upward, near the top.

Route

Take a jeep up from Mestia to the Cross then on up to the highest of the summer pasture huts. This cuts out three hours of slog – giving you (or at least me) enough puff to take on this high altitude walk. Beyond the hut (beside a small tarn) the track degrades into a series of parallel paths. Standing at the bottom you can clearly see your destination – a short flattish ridge one kilometre straight above. With binoculars it's possible to make out a small cross on the summit. The route is clear – following a ridge leading toward the Guli pass to the left, then climbing the final steep flanks to the Coruldi ridge. There is another route to add variety - and stunning views of Banguriani and Darigora; or if the ridge is too windy. After some twenty minutes up from the hut a smaller path branches off to the right, away from the more direct ridge route. Follow this and the climb becomes easier and calmer. Also, after about thirty more minutes, you encounter a small spring, which with a bit of digging allows bottles to be filled. Although accompanied by parallel cow paths the way is pretty logical – take the biggest going up. Eventually it winds round and up to the left to a series of small lakes. At the far end of the last lake the ridge is clearly visible – which you pick up for the final long push up to the Coruldi ridge. Here life becomes more tricky. The way steepens and the ground deteriorates into small shards of coloured, and endlessly slipping slate. But keep your bearings straight for the ridge just below and to the right of the cross – which should be visible now with the naked eye. Patches of snow make this climb easier (if colder). The feet slip back less on the compacting snow. A mixture of both is ideal – up on the snow, down on the slate. After some considerable climbing a small plateau opens out. Directly above is the Coruldi ridge - the Coruldi Plateau is slightly to the left, behind the peak with the cross. If you're making the walk after the first October snows, or before the final July melt – you will almost certainly now be facing a snow walk, intermixed with patches of crumbling slate (gloves, sunglasses and a windcheater with hood are advised). The final 100 metres up to the ridge is very steep with some scrambling. The rock is loose so be careful and make certain *nobody is directly above or below you*. However just when it all starts to feel too much, the top of the ridge suddenly arrives, with one of the finest walker's views in the Caucasus – described above. A great place for lunch.

Down. Quickest is the way you came avoiding the lakes, staying on the ridge all the way. Some may not still have the jeep – it's more expensive to have the driver stay up the whole day. If so, either just follow the jeep track back down, or choose one of the Walk 42 routes down.

NOTE:

The super fit can do this walk all the way from Mestia in one day. IE combining Walks 42 and 43. Only attempt this in July or August when the days are longest. I've only met one person who made it (I tried once and failed).

WHERE WALKERS FEAR TO TREAD

Managed to convince my host Gia to drive me up to the Cross summit above Mestia, (the walk's start), in his Niva. As we set off I noticed no one joined us. Normally in Svaneti to leave a car high in the mountains unattended, for minutes, let alone hours, is unheard of. 'Car OK up?' I asked tentatively. 'OK,' came the flat reply. Then I realised why – the high alpine village was now deserted after the first October snow a week earlier. All the potatoes had been harvested, the sheep and cattle were down, huts abandoned until the spring. Nobody but mad dogs, the odd hunter and Englishmen would go now. First we detoured across town, past the recently burnt-out police station ('yes, we know who did it…'), past the 'Swimming Pool,' a dammed-up stream beside the road, to the airport with its frequently-grazed grass runway, then back and up the mountain. At the Cross we hit strong sunshine and I peered out the Niva window hoping to see the top of Ushba. Although still swathed in white cloud – we could see the upper needles of Chatin Tau and all of Daligora. A good sign. We both agreed that finally, after four summitless days, Ushba would reveal himself in full twin-headed glory…

Five minutes later, up on the plateau Gia parked the car beside the final deserted hut – about the size of a garden shed. It perched perilously alone on a treeless plateau at 2300 metres, surrounded by gaping skies and empty valleys. To the north, one ominous black trunk of rock disappeared into the clouds – Ushba South. How on earth it stayed on this ridge in the vicious prevailing winds, when surely just one puff would flatten its playing card walls…?

We locked the Niva and I walked to the path. It felt strange standing up on a ridge – that on my previous attempt at the Coruldi plateau two months earlier, had only been gained after three hours of sweat. Then I'd only managed about half as far again - still two hours below the ridge - before running out of time. But now it was only 9.15am. Slanting sunlight sliced across the Mestia valley, hit everything at near right-angles; the air was still and crisp, clouds thinning on all sides. The perfect day – only a matter of minutes now before the veil blew away and there would be Ushba, complete and smiling….I surveyed our goal, the flat Coruldi ridge clearly visible in the burning sunlight one kilo-metre higher in the sky. It still looked very high.

We set off, directly up the ridge, not deviating toward the spring (contrary to my route advice). Gia borrowed my binoculars and said 'Many snow, many snow!' but kept on walking. For, while snow lay deep and drift-ed on the high-pasture slopes, it had been blown from the ridge lip to leave a twelve inch strip of bare earth beside a great drop – our path. We walked on happy for this small blessing. The air remained incredibly still for such an exposed position – everything augured well for that perfect day. In my mind I joked – imagin-ing hurrying down in a blizzard, repeating the words to Lou Reed's 'Perfect Day... drinking sangria in the park...'

We passed the lakes with only a minimum of snow walking – then started the serious climb up the steep-ening flanks of the Coruldi ridge. Now more and more snow which I strenuously avoided in my semi-porous walker's shoes. Gia, wearing Wellingtons plunged into the white powder at every opportunity and encour-aged me to follow. I of course avoided it, but soon found my progress amounting to one large step for-ward then half a step slip-back in the shale. 'Follow me; better!' he shouted but still I resisted until finally a large patch of snow spread out ahead. I'd no choice. As soon as I placed my feet in his footsteps I found progress speeding up, Of course! The snow compacted to build a mini-step, unlike the shale which avalanched back on itself. Much to my surprise, this dangerous, slippery cold substance made the climb considerably easier. I assume common knowledge to mountaineers, but to this walker, a great discovery. Fortunately I'd thought to bring my two dollar sunglasses, which pre-vented partial snow blindness. But the orange, polarised plastic turned the world into a crepuscular film set in which nothing seemed real.

Then something unexpected happened; the sun went in. How, after such a fabulous, becalmed start? Not a puff of wind up our exposed ridge, then clouds piling in from nowhere. Gia shook his head grimly. 'Today much snow.' But then the sun returned, then disap-peared, beginning a game with my sunglasses, that had to come off and on repeatedly. Meanwhile the wind picked up surreptitiously.

But this I hardly noticed as altitude had started to kick in. We were approaching 3000 metres – my speed slowed up, breath heaved. The words to a punk song repeated stupidly in my brain 'Beat on the brat, beat on the brat with a baseball bat,' then finally we arrived on a small plateau. Not the Coruldi, but at least its tiny cross stood out considerably larger against the sky.

Not far now… except that ahead lay pure snow and a very steep slope threatening to turn this walk into a climb. We set off like two mountaineers – without gear – across the wide white expanse and were soon climbing steeply. The snow footholds for the most part held – occasionally giving way to sink my leg in beyond the knee, forcing me to fall forward into the hillside lest I turn into a giant snowball racing to the bottom.

But thanks to my orange glasses, everything was fine. None of this was really happening. I lay in bed back at home dreaming all this. We crossed the slope and found ourselves on a very steep, rocky incline. A number of times I had to resort to three, sometimes four legs, hauling myself cautiously round unsteady boulders, testing each rock carefully as some gave away. Gia continued on about ten metres above, them suddenly came a crack. I saw him lurch forward as his left leg dislodged a huge boulder. He stayed on the slope without any difficulty but the boulder crashed down, spinning and crunching against the snow just three metres ahead of me. A stark warning, which I vaguely registered inside my tangerine dream….

We continued on, now careful he never climbed directly above. Then, just when it all seemed too much suddenly he shouted down 'We're here!' and disappeared from view. In a burst of new vigour I joined him on the ridge top - to confront one of the most spectacular views I've ever seen.

A completely new world spread out. One kilometre of open space then directly below two huge glaciers tumbling from the clouds. Snow and ice lay in a jagged, angry carpet of crevasses, cliffs and falls. Both about a kilometre wide and joining somewhere out of sight below. Directly ahead stood the 4368 metre Chatin Tau – wafting its savage struts of rock in and out of cloud. Behind that lay the angry cliffs of Ushba, the siren-call to so many climbers - that nine months later would kill one of my, and so many people's, most treasured Georgian friends, Zaal Kikodze.

Immediately I felt the sheer hostility of this place… Human beings did not belong here at all. Even to see it seemed to break the rules. I felt we'd be punished for this trespass – would probably have to escape. Briefly I'd become a walker transgressing into the terrain of climbers. Indeed no sooner had we unpacked lunch than small chunks of white crystal began appearing on our khajapuri. At first I thought some kind of salt from inside the bag – but as it heaped up it quickly became apparent - a strange crystalline snow. Soon it was bouncing joyfully off my windcheater, gathering in my camera case like mini Styrofoam balls. Gloves were now required and I noticed my feet now froze inside their sodden shoes – indeed my toes had lost all sensation. Removing shoes and socks I massaged them back to a partial life – incurring sharp pain as they thawed. Now the snow was dancing viciously against everything and the view ahead, dimming. I cursed I hadn't taken a picture on arrival – and prayed the snow would stop. Gia looked up at the sky and said 'Very much snow…' But I kept eating determinedly, feeling my feet lose their pain, become feet again. Then suddenly a miracle happened. The snow stopped and a tiny crack of blue appeared in the sky directly above. Instantly a ray of sunlight shot down and hit the Chalati glacier below. Desperately I fumbled for my camera, but by the time the lens cap was off, the sun had disappeared. I ran off a few shots anyway noticing how cold my fingers had become - then realised why. The wind had picked up; then the snow began again, drilling against my skin like needles. My camera case started filling up with Styrofoam. I shook it out and turned to Gia. He looked anxious, but never suggested we leave. He had delivered me to this fantastic place as promised – even if the sky had turned grey and the view vanished.

I raised my hood to defend against the needles which banged against the plastic turning my head into a kettle drum. No doubt about it – we were being kicked out. To test the wind speed I spat - and the spittle shot out of my mouth at 90 degrees. Rapidly we packed the lunch and set off down. By now the drilling had reached gale force. I couldn't turn my face into the wind due to the pain of needles. I saw Gia's face, now bright red, but fortunately our footsteps served as a guide rail and soon we were way down on the lower Coruldi flanks sliding through the slate in long, bounding leaps. The moment we hit the ridge below the lakes, the sun burst out again to welcome the heroes' return. For hadn't we just returned from a place we walkers should never normally go.

USHGULI

INTRODUCTION/HISTORY

If Mestia is a fine example of how Georgia's culture survived through the centuries, then Usguli is its secret heart for... how could anyone find it? Georgians claim Ushguli as the highest, permanently occupied village group in Europe at 2200 metres. It's also one of the oldest; the bases of some towers date to pre-Christian times. Historically a remarkable place, not to mention its fine 11th-12th century towers. In 1993 it was declared a World Heritage Site by UNESCO due to its antiquity and fantastically remote atmosphere. Some remoteness disappeared with the new mobile mast - placed in the most prominent position, near the main watch-tower. Composed of four villages (the main one is Chajhashi), Ushguli contains two small museums, one in a tower and one in a house. Opening is not reliable, or sometimes even possible. Walks however are – and numerous. Here I'm afraid is only one. Homestay accommodation is always available, and often lifts in local Niva jeeps.

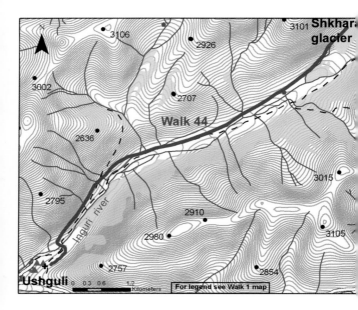

LOCATOIN

The Ushguli villages are about two hours' jeep ride from Mestia – if you don't stop (too far to walk in one day). But the way up is very beautiful and interesting, with the villages of Ipari and Kvala with their famous 12th century churches (and fine frescos). The only way up is by jeep.

Ushguli

Walk 44

The SHKHARA GLACIER

Start/end - Ushguli
Type - Single direction, return
Date - June to September
Time - 6 hours
Upward climb - 300 metres
Max elevation - 2500 metres
Grade - Easy
Mobile signal - At start only

Summary

This fairly easy walk takes you to the base of Georgia's highest mountain, Shkhara (5068m) – giving splendid views of this giant much of the way. The walk itself is longish but for the most part flat, running along a wide, mostly treeless valley. On the final section you walk up beside a river running down from the glacier. The goal is the glacier tongue itself – not as spectacular as Chalati – but a simple glance upwards at the majestic cathedrals of

Mt Shkhara

rock and snow lifting straight up into the sky. easily compensates. The walk can be shortened and intensified by jeeping up the valley – missing out the less interesting first hour and a half of valley (preferable).

Route

Walk up out of the last Ushguli village along the jeep track toward the Lamara Church and tower - the highest stone building in the valley. Beyond it the track dips down slightly – and picks up the river from the Shkhara glacier. This is your guide all the way. After about 20 minutes along the track you encounter the first and only significant obstacle on the walk – a ford of the river. Usually there is a narrow plank bridge up to the left. If the summer floods have washed it away – then nothing for it but take off the shoes, role up the trouser legs and encounter some bracing glacial water. But it's a short distance and a good stick will help for balance. A quick wipe down and you're on the way – up the now wide, treeless valley. Follow the jeep track all the way. This is the least eventful part of the walk, but the looming snowy massif of Shkhara makes you forget the routine. An hour later the jeep track sort of peters out, or

rather seems to merge with the river. At this point stay on the left hand side of the river, following it all the way up to the point where it divides (another river meets it from the right). Bear left up the valley towards the now visible Shkhara glacier. There is a rough path that meanders parallel to the river, on the left hand side. You can also climb along the river itself, leaping between the wonderfully red-oxidised boulders. When arriving at the glacier tongue – remember the warning from Walk 1 – do *not* stand directly under the tongue of the glacier (boulders can race down without warning).

Back. Simply retrace your steps – not forgetting to turn round frequently to catch the receding, but still splendid views of Shkhara in the changing light.

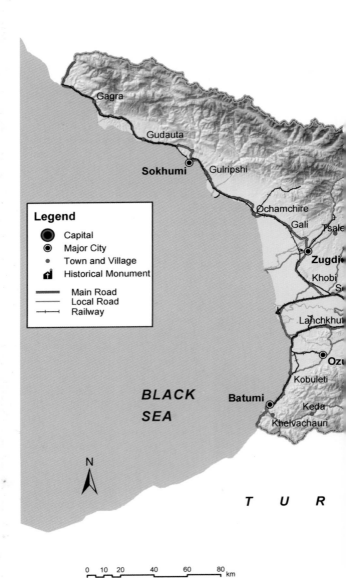